Extreme Crisis Leadership

This concise handbook presents a framework to help leaders across sectors understand what their role should be in an extreme crisis and supplements this understanding with practical advice.

Leadership is often presented as a kind of mastery—but no single person can master an extreme crisis event such as the COVID-19 pandemic. Leaders need a workable resource based on research and experience that can be accessed quickly and referenced easily to effectively handle crises and mitigate repercussions: This handbook is that resource. It begins with diagnostic tools to identify crisis types and leadership roles, then presents an easy-to-use matrix framework that allows readers to focus on the specific example-based section that best fits their role and the kind of crisis they face.

This handbook is accessible to leaders at all levels, from shift supervisors and emergency responders to CEOs and government executives. It will be an essential ready reference for any leader who might expect to encounter an extreme crisis, as well as for those who would not have foreseen themselves in such a situation.

Dr. Charles A. Casto is a safety and regulatory professional with over 45 years of experience, including executive, regulatory, technical, and operational roles. Dr. Casto is the recipient of both the US Presidential Distinguished Award (2012) and the US Meritorious Rank Award (2009) and he served at the US Nuclear Regulatory Commission (NRC) for 28 years. His international experience as an extreme crisis leader includes having led the integrated US Government and NRC effort in Japan during and after the Fukushima nuclear accident, representing the US Government to the Japanese Prime Minister's Cabinet.

Extreme Crisis Leadership

A Handbook for Leading Through the Unpredictable

Charles A. Casto

Routledge
Taylor & Francis Group

NEW YORK AND LONDON

First published 2023
by Routledge
605 Third Avenue, New York, NY 10158

and by Routledge
4 Park Square, Milton Park, Abingdon, Oxon, OX14 4RN

Routledge is an imprint of the Taylor & Francis Group, an informa business

© 2023 Charles A. Casto

Library of Congress Cataloging-in-Publication Data
Names: Casto, Charles A, author.
Title: Extreme crisis leadership : a handbook to managing the unpredictable / Charles A Casto.
Description: 1 Edition. | New York, NY : Routledge, 2023. | Includes bibliographical references and index. |
Identifiers: LCCN 2022027823 | ISBN 9781032266350 (hardback) | ISBN 9781032266336 (paperback) | ISBN 9781003289180 (ebook)
Subjects: LCSH: Crisis management. | Leadership. | COVID-19 Pandemic, 2020---Influence.
Classification: LCC HD49 .C387 2023 | DDC 658.4/056--dc23/eng/20220725
LC record available at https://lccn.loc.gov/2022027823

ISBN: 9781032266350 (hbk)
ISBN: 9781032266336 (pbk)
ISBN: 9781003289180 (ebk)

DOI: 10.4324/9781003289180

Typeset in Bembo
by KnowledgeWorks Global Ltd.

Dedication

The inspiration for this handbook came from a friend's experience leading through a cyber-attack on the State of Georgia computer systems. She used my book Station Blackout - Inside the Fukushima Nuclear Disaster as a guide in responding to that crisis. From her experience, I thought creating a simple handbook for crisis leaders was worthwhile.

This handbook was written for you for those leaders who find themselves in an extreme crisis without a clear path. I hope it provides you with a more straightforward path through the crisis.

Contents

CHAPTER 1

Introduction

We're accustomed to thinking about leadership as a kind of mastery—of people, resources, information, and decisions. Reality often falls short of this ideal, but nothing guts it as completely as an extreme crisis. These are the events, like Apollo 13 or the Fukushima nuclear disaster, that seem too huge and too horrible to plan for. They catch us flat-footed, smashing normal protocols and threatening not only the event site but also the wider community.

No single person can master an event like this. Anyone who tries to control 100%, or even 50%, of the crisis space will control none of it. For leaders who strive for mastery, this experience is both disorienting and demoralizing.

Once leaders recognize the limits of their impact, they are free to consider the real nature of their contribution: *What part of the crisis do leaders have power over? What problems can they work on directly? Who can be influenced? What information and resources can leaders access, or offer to* others? *If leaders can't fix it all—what can they do?*

This handbook offers a model for thinking through these questions, helping leaders of all stripes understand what their role should be in an extreme crisis. The theoretical framework will be supplemented with practical advice based on Dr. Charles A. Casto's extensive interviews with global crisis leaders, his book on the Fukushima nuclear disaster, and a co-authored Harvard Business Review Article—*How the Other Fukushima Survived*. This handbook is a practical accompaniment to those references.[1]

Inevitably, response organizations will have hierarchies; however, in extreme crisis situations, all responders must know how to lead, regardless of rank. This handbook is for members of, or people who work with, the emergency operations center at organizations that may face an extreme crisis. These are the individuals who prevent, mitigate, prepare for, and respond to crises. They carry out emergency management and ensure the continuity of a crisis response operation by giving or receiving orders.

DOI: 10.4324/9781003289180-1

This handbook is a workable resource based on research and experience that can be accessed quickly and referenced easily to effectively handle crises and mitigate repercussions. 'The abstract given in the beginning of each chapter of the handbook provides background information about that chapter that will make the *Crisis Leadership* chapters clearer:

- **Chapter 2:** *Key Terms and Concepts* explores commonly used phrases and important ideas that form the basis for each crisis type's bespoke response strategy.
- **Chapter 3:** *Crisis Types* provides information on how to "diagnose" what crisis situation the reader is facing so that they may more readily access the appropriate *Extreme Crisis Leadership* chapter.
- **Chapter 4:** *Cross-Case Issues* provides an overview of topics that are relevant regardless of crisis type, and that will be tailored to fit each of the crises described in *Extreme Crisis Leadership* chapters.

Readers in the midst of a crisis should reference the flowchart in the next chapter to determine what crisis they are in, and quickly reference the relevant sections accordingly. For leaders with more time, it is recommended to read the handbook chronologically.

The rest of the handbook is divided into four crisis types, with each subsequent chapter increasing in severity:

- Chapter 5: *Surprise Crises—Black Elephants Crises*
- Chapter 6: *Failure Crises—Gray Rhino Crises*
- Chapter 7: *Catastrophic Crises—Gray Swans Crises*
- Chapter 8: *Super-Catastrophic Crises—Black Swans Crises*

These animal names are not academic terms. They are explained both in Chapter 3 and in Chapters 5 through 8—do not worry if they seem unclear now.

Each chapter contains a case study exemplifying the crisis type, which will provide a frame of reference as the academic literature is applied to practical leadership strategies in further subsections of:

- **Situational Context**—The crisis and its circumstances.
  - Including *surprise, failure, catastrophic,* or *extreme* crises.
- **Sensemaking**—How leaders understand the crisis situation.
  - Including *updating, enacted, meta-thinking,* or *common perspective* mental models.

- **Decision Making**—How leaders decide what to do with their understanding.
  - Including *experience, recognition, functional*, or *unified* processes.
- **Crisis Response**—How leaders act on their decisions.
  - Including *cooperative, complex, systems*, or *integrated* actions.
- **Leadership**—The way leaders act on their decisions.
  - Including *adaptive, non-linear, situational*, and *warrior* leadership styles.

These larger concepts are further defined and explored in Chapter 2, Key Terms and Concepts, to lay the groundwork for each *Extreme Crisis Leadership* chapter's specific guidance. The individual styles are expanded upon in Chapters 5 through 8, respectively.

While leadership cannot be mastered, it can be prepared for and practiced. The goal of this handbook is to provide leaders with a reference so that in even the most daunting of circumstances—extreme crises—they can act and to mitigate, controlling enough of the response to return their organization to the status quo as quickly as possible.

NOTE

1 Station Blackout—Inside the Fukushima Nuclear Disaster and Recovery—Radius Press, December 2018, ISBN-10: 1635764025; ISBN-13: 978-1635764024. Crisis Management—How the Other Fukushima Plant Survived by Ranjay Gulati, Charles Casto, and Charlotte Krontiris HBR (July–August 2014).

CHAPTER 2

Key terms and concepts

COMMONLY USED TERMS

This handbook will use a variety of terms that hold a specific meaning in the context of this guide. There will be more terms explained throughout the hand book, but the most used are defined and described below.

Disaster/Crisis

Technically, the terms *disaster* and *crisis* are defined differently: *Disasters* occur when external hazards and organizational vulnerabilities combine with a lack of planning and use of resources, while *crises* are abnormal situations that present high risks and may trigger rapid policy changes because of threatened trust in governments or authorities. However, there is significant overlap between disasters and crises, with blurred lines causing mainstream academic literature to treat these words as synonyms.

Therefore, this handbook will use the terms disaster and crisis interchangeably. In this context, disasters/crises will encompass extreme technical or natural events, such as cyberattacks or nuclear meltdowns. This handbook will *not* include reputational or corporate crises, like losing market share, in its definition.

Leader

This is a handbook for extreme crisis *leader*ship, so the terms *leader* and *responder* will often be used interchangeably. Inevitably, response organizations will have hierarchies; however, in extreme crisis situations, all responders must know how to lead, regardless of rank.

DOI: 10.4324/9781003289180-2

In this handbook, *responders* are members of, or people who work with, the emergency operations center at organizations that come up against an extreme crisis. These are all of the individuals who prevent, prepare for, mitigate, and respond to crises. They carry out emergency management and ensure the continuity of a crisis response operation by giving or receiving orders.

Relationships between responders will be illustrated using the terms *leaders* and *teams*, with *leaders* describing those typically of higher rank and giving orders and *teams* describing those typically of lower rank and receiving them. Even further distinctions will occasionally be made, referring to some teams as *on-site* responders. These individuals are at the location where the crisis happened or is happening, and their leaders might either be on-site as well or supervising from an off-site location.

Familiarity

Before a crisis occurs, organizations operate in a state of *familiarity*, or *status quo*. Day-to-day operations unaffected by any adverse occurrences are familiar, meaning that once a crisis occurs, leaders' number one goal is to return the situation to a state of familiarity, or a crisis that can be mitigated using traditional crisis management protocol.

Media res

When a leader is amid a disaster, they are in *media res*. Throughout the hand book, this term will be used interchangeably with the phrase *on the ground* and *crisis situation* to describe the settings in which a crisis is taking place.

KEY CONCEPTS

Each of the following *Crisis Leadership* chapters will be broken down into five subsections: *Situational Context, Sensemaking, Decision Making, Crisis Response,* and *Leadership*. Brief explanations of these sections are provided below.

Situational context sets the backdrop composed of the crisis and its circumstances, which the leaders must strive to *make sense* of. Once they begin to understand the crisis, leaders must *decide* what to do and then begin to *respond*. Throughout, strong *leadership* skills allow for the successful implementation of a crisis response strategy.

SITUATIONAL CONTEXT

Triggering events form crises, creating conditions that depart from familiarity. These conditions, or *situational contexts*, provide a backdrop for the crisis and its response, helping to categorize and group crisis types. The situational context consists of the triggering event and the capacity of the organization to respond to it; the crisis is the specific event happening within this context. All crisis types covered in this handbook can be categorized within three broad situational contexts, *routine*, *extreme*, and *dangerous*:

- **Routine situations** are those in which the organization can predict the event and can respond. These are also known as *fathomable* events, or events within the realm of imagination for which one can be prepared. Routine situations include *surprise events* that exceed the severity of routine events but are still fathomable. In these situations, the organization can expand its abilities to meet the response demands. More information on routine situations can be found in Chapter 5, on Black Elephant crises.

  For example, a fire department may routinely extinguish housefires with one truck; an entire apartment block ablaze may come as a surprise but an event still well within its ability to handle. In this situation, a fire department may expand its capabilities by using *all* their fire trucks to meet the response demands.

- **Extreme situations** are those events in which the severity of the event exceeds what was expected and prepared for. Extreme crises surpass an organization's routine, or practiced, ability to respond. However, *unlike* surprise situations, extreme events exceed the organization's ability to expand its capabilities and require assistance from outside organizations to respond. More information on extreme situations can be found in Chapter 6, on Gray Rhinos, and Chapter 7, on Gray Swans.

  For example, a fire department may be able to put out an apartment block fire by bringing in more trucks, but a building collapsing in flames may require even more trucks and manpower. The firefighters may call on other emergency response organizations to send in resources to respond.

- **Dangerous contexts** include situations that greatly exceed an organization's abilities and include conditions where the lives of those involved in the response could be in jeopardy. Often, these events combine multiple extreme situations at once. More information on extreme situations can be found in Chapter 8 on Black Swans.

  For example, firefighters may put their own lives in danger when responding to a terror attack like 9/11. This situation combined multiple extreme situations: An unfathomable plane crash and a building collapse followed by *another* crash and collapse. This event greatly exceeded one fire department's ability to respond and put all responders' lives at risk.

SENSEMAKING

Sensemaking is how a leader processes the situation around them in order to begin making choices to resolve it and return to familiarity. Though these tips will be explored in Chapters 3–9 on a crisis-by-crisis basis, below are general recommendations on how to effectively digest a situation:

- **Look for clarity**—in *media res*, take a step back and try to find clear markers of *what* is happening, *where* it is happening, and *who* it is happening to. This will lay the groundwork for a strategy to resolve the situation. Try to find *situational interpreters,* or people who can clearly explain the situation, to assist at this stage.
   For example, when a firefighter arrives on the scene of a house fire, they must determine the size of the fire and the number of people that might be inside. Someone that was inside the burning building can act as a situational interpreter to provide this information.
- **Set priorities**—in a crisis, there will be many challenges. Decide which are the most important to tackle first to make the crisis response more manageable.
   For example, firefighters must decide the biggest risks to those inside and to their team when determining which areas to hose down or which rooms to enter.
- **Set a "battle rhythm"**—immediately set a pace for action. In a crisis, sensemaking must coincide with decision-making; be prepared to act and to think simultaneously.
   For example, firefighters might set a pace of how quickly hoses will be turned on and rescuers will enter the building.
- **Set a "goal post" for leaders**—assess the situation and determine best and worst outcomes. Inform the leadership team accordingly and be prepared to measure success of response throughout against these outcomes.
   For example, firefighters need to determine how many lives or structures can realistically be saved.

DECISION-MAKING

Once a leader has made sense of the situational context and crisis, decision-making is what they choose to do, including but not limited to: Information that they search for, commands that they give, and actions that they take. There are key tenants to effective crisis-response decision-making that will be explored in more depth throughout the handbook:

- **Anchor facts**—be strategic about what is shared and do not say more than is known for sure.

  🏠   For example, firefighters must be sure that there are people inside to rescue before entering a burning building.

- **Watch for "rabbit holes"**—be aware of potential distractions that take away from effective crisis response.

  🏠   For example, firefighters must ignore distractions like a crowd forming to watch the building burn.

- **Add value rather than complexity**—be sure to avoid "random" ideas. Different proposals can cause confusion, so take clear, decisive action driven by data and/or strategy.

  🏠   For example, firefighters must act instead of overthinking the best ways to enter the building and complicating the response.

- **Let the data "bake"**—if there is not a need to act, then do not act. Allow the data to sit until a clearer perspective develops.

  🏠   For example, firefighters might allow a clearer perspective of the extent of the fire to develop before determining the best plan of response.

- **Interrogate the data**—do not let single data points or models drive strategy and ask questions about the data itself as well as those who supply the data.

  🏠   For example, firefighters taking on big blazes might talk to on-scene actors about how long the flame has been burning and what the conditions are like inside.

- **Understand available technologies and understand information failure**—know what technologies are available as solutions and be aware of their limitations. Be aware that information technology can and will fail.

  🏠   For example, firefighters are aware that heat sensors may not always be accurate and that other measures of heat to determine the source of the fire, like survivor testimonies, should be used.

- **Act quickly**—the speed of decision-making should roughly correlate with the speed of the event. This will prevent cascading crises, or situations that escalate because events pile on top of one another without decisive intervention.

🏠 For example, firefighters in the face of a blaze act quickly by combatting the flames faster than they can spread.

• **Delegate with authority**—designate a decision-maker to be the director of action. Having one voice to make decisions reduces confusion.

🏠 For example, firefighters trust the fire chief to issue orders.

CRISIS RESPONSE

Once leaders understand the crisis and decide what to do about it, then the crisis response can begin. Crisis response constitutes not only the strategic actions taken when a situation occurs, but also *how* those actions are taken and *who* they are taken with. This encompasses the planned and strategic activities of an organization as they tackle a crisis, including their on-site capabilities and the potential for involvement from parties outside of the crisis site. Crisis response relates to the outcome of a disaster in that a successful response will mitigate or resolve events. However, there are significant factors that can influence an organization's crisis response:

• **Latent organizational weaknesses** have a negative impact on crisis response because in extreme crisis situations, even the smallest underlying organizational deficiencies can have massive consequences.

🏠 For example, newer firefighters may not perform their jobs as efficiently and might respond more slowly, which for more widespread fires will mean more damage and extreme circumstances.

• **Resilience expansion** can reduce the complexity of a crisis response. This means that crisis responders can limit the chaos in their response by thinking and acting flexibly and being able to "bounce back" from any setbacks.

🏠 For example, the usual fire retardant used by a fire department might be unavailable or the team might be short-staffed during a fire, so the team finds a suitable material replacement and calls on other departments for help as quickly as possible. The sooner they can overcome these setbacks, the sooner they can refocus on the task at hand.

• **Communicating changes** throughout the crisis response is crucial, especially as plans are updated with new data and strategies.

🏠 For example, if it is no longer safe for firefighters to enter a burning building, that change in strategy should be communicated as quickly as possible to reduce risks and keep the team on track to save what they can.

As crises escalate, crisis response becomes less important because logistics and management techniques make way for instinctual and adaptive leadership. Chapters 3–9 will outline how leaders can continue to incorporate crisis response strategies to try to mitigate damage.

LEADERSHIP

Leadership encompasses not only how responders take actions in *media res* in relation to the response team they are working with, but also how a responder prepares for a crisis. This hand book will explore crisis-specific on-the-ground leadership techniques further in Chapters 3–9, but below are methods for improving leadership and crisis management skills *before* a crisis begins:

- **Find trusted mentors**—form professional relationships with people that can be trusted both inside and outside of the workplace.
  - For example, a fire captain may find mentors in retired fire captains or military officials who have more, broader experience and whom they can lean on when advice is needed.
- **Continue to learn**—find opportunities to be curious about leadership strategies outside of work, such as attending lectures, listening to podcasts, or reading books.
  - For example, a fire captain may attend a talk by a motivational speaker that may inspire leadership or teamwork at the firehouse.
- **Remain calm while managing day-to-day crises**—this practice will help sensemaking and decision-making if/when an extreme crisis situation arises.
  - For example, during routine crises like small housefires, leaders should remain calm and collected, follow standard protocol, and practice strong teamwork.
- **Recognize that preparedness drills drive out both uncertainty and innovation**—while practicing crisis response drills regularly is important, good leaders are acutely aware that these practices limit innovative thinking in a crisis situation.
  - For example, firefighters should be well-versed in standard procedures, but remain flexible enough to adapt to extreme situations. Fire captains should be aware of and vocalize this shortcoming during each training.

- **Practice *meta thinking*—**think about thinking and be prepared to analyze what might be needed to make sense of a situation and/or develop actions.

  For example, firefighters should consistently practice forecasting what decisions they might have to make in a certain situation (e.g., *What do I need to think about to decide if I enter this building? What will my criteria be for calling on other fire departments for assistance?*)

This is not an exhaustive list of terms; many more new concepts will be introduced throughout the hand book. It is recommended that readers refer back to this terminology as often as necessary to make sense of their crisis. Chapter 3 will discuss each crisis type in turn and will help the reader diagnose what type of crisis they might be facing.

CHAPTER 3

Crisis types

Crises are abnormal situations that occur when hazards and vulnerabilities combine with a lack of planning and/or appropriate resource use. For example, in the 2011 Fukushima nuclear disaster, an earthquake and tsunami (hazards) and a nuclear plant near the Japanese coast (vulnerability) combined with a lack of planning for a potential nuclear meltdown to create an extreme, unfathomable crisis. While all disasters are not this extreme, crises of all severities present high risks to the response teams, infrastructure, and surrounding populations.

Each crisis is different and there is no unified theory of extreme crisis leadership, meaning that there is no "right" way to handle a disaster. There are, however, more appropriate ways to respond based on the severity of the crisis; these bespoke responses can help mitigate damage and help organizations return to the status quo as quickly as possible.

This handbook introduces a system of categorization that can help leaders prepare for potential disasters and quickly identify the crisis type they are in so that they can respond most effectively. While no two crises are the same—and often events will blur lines and cross neat, categorical boundaries—the main crisis types identified in academia will be outlined below. Chapters 4–9 will use this framework to examine the leadership strategies and characteristics that best suit each crisis type. However, remember that these are only rough outlines, and it might be useful to reference other chapters to tailor a crisis response most effectively in *media res*.

CLASSIFYING CRISES

Crises differ in the level of *information* available, the potential *consequences* of the event, and the *pre-crisis actions* taken to effectively prevent or solve the problem before the event occurs. These attributes—information,

DOI: 10.4324/9781003289180-3

consequences, and pre-crisis actions—are what set a house fire apart from a nuclear disaster.

Crises become more severe as less information is known about the event, the consequences of the event present more risks to the responders and their community, and as responders have done less pre-crisis preparation. Though they are linked and often correlate, these attributes Table 3.1 define imitations of the response more than they define the crisis itself.

According to the Casto Pandemonium Curve, less information leads to more chaos. So, when less information about the event is known, the response is harder to execute. If the consequences of the event present risks to the responders themselves or their communities, responders are more likely to be emotionally limited in their response. If responders have not adequately prepared for a crisis, they are less likely to respond effectively. These attributes vary and boundaries can be blurred, but when applied to crisis situations, these categorizations can help inform the response.

The *Crisis Leadership* portion of the hand book will be divided into crisis types based on these attributes:

- **White Swan** crises occur when information about the situation is known beforehand, the safety consequences to the responders themselves and the surrounding community are low, and response organizations have taken and continue to take actions to mitigate or control the crisis. Because these crises are routine (and not extreme), they will not be discussed further in this handbook.

   For example, a house is on fire. The local fire department has full knowledge about fires and about the specific area beforehand. It has safety equipment, and the fire is contained in one location, so the community

TABLE 3.1 Crisis Situation Attributes

	Information	Consequences	Pre-Crisis Actions
White Swan	Known	Low	Act
Black Elephant	Known	Moderate	Mitigate
Gray Rhino	Known	High	Muddle
Gray Swan	Likely known	Extreme	Deny
Black Swan	Unknown	Unfathomable	None

is not at risk. It routinely puts out housefires, so it is well prepared to control the flames.

- **Black Elephant** crises occur when information about the situation is known or available during the event, the safety consequences to the responders themselves and the surrounding community are moderate, and responders have acted to mitigate the crisis before it begins.

  For example, a space shuttle has deployed but is losing oxygen quickly. The command center on the ground is able to gather information from the astronauts, and the responders themselves and the wider community are not at high risk. Before the space shuttle launched, precautions to mitigate oxygen loss were taken.

- **Gray Rhino** crises occur when information about the situation is known or available, but the consequences are high to the responders themselves and the surrounding community, so responders muddle, or are confused on whether they should act, before the event occurs.

  For example, a superstorm is headed toward a major city. There is information about the storm's path and potential damage. The responders and their communities are at risk of flooding, extreme infrastructure damage, and even death. However, the impending storm is so overwhelming that responders cannot decide if they should, or even how to, how to respond.

- **Gray Swan** crises occur when information about the situation is likely to be known in advance, the consequences for responders and the wider community are extreme, and the chances of this event are so low that responders deny that the situation might ever occur.

  For example, an oil rig is on fire. Days before, decisions were made that made it more difficult to detect a gas leak, but the oil rig owners thought the chance of a gas leak leading to the fire was so small that they did not prepare to respond.

- **Black Swan** crises occur when information about the situation is entirely *un*known, the consequences to responders and surrounding community are unfathomable, and responders are so surprised by the event that no action has been taken to prepare for it and there is no guide on how to proceed.

  For example, an earthquake has caused a tsunami near a nuclear reactor site, wiping out the reactor's resources and threatening nuclear meltdown. The responders have never experienced anything so dangerous with so little manpower and there is no predetermined guide on how to proceed.

CASCADING EVENTS

Events can exist between categorizations, or in multiple categories at once. Crises can also move between crisis types; a crisis may *cascade*, escalating to another as events build, or *de-escalate*, as more information is known, and more actions are taken. Figure 3.1 shows how crises can move between crisis types over time as information is lost/learned, consequences are heightened/ lowered, and response preparation is decreased/increased. While not every crisis is going to cascade or de-escalate, it is important to keep in mind the factors that can cause it to do so.

Crisis types are only meant to act as a guide so that leadership response can be measured against a rubric, but these are not necessarily set in stone or one-size-fits-all. The "gray area" above demonstrates the space where events may exist in between crisis types. Here, leaders should use their discretion to determine which crisis most closely matches their situation, referencing crisis response strategies from the crisis on either side.

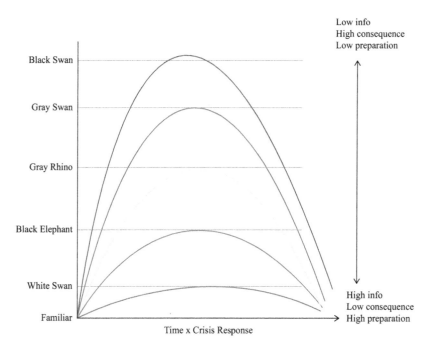

FIGURE 3.1 Time × Crisis Response

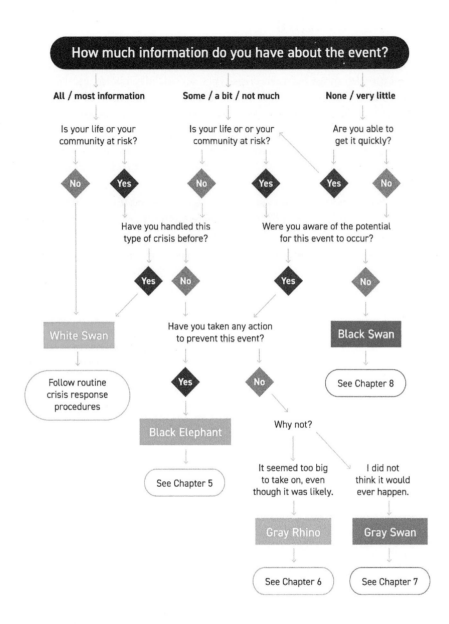

FLOWCHART 3.1 Crisis Response Assessment

For example, a plane has struck a flock of birds and engine power is lost. Information about the event is known, the consequences to responders and to the wider community are moderate, but the possibility of this event occurring was so small that crisis preparedness teams denied it could happen. Here, leaders might place the crisis between a Black Elephant and Gray Swan and refer to each chapter for bespoke leadership strategies.

What crisis am I in?

Flowchart 3.1 can be used for leaders in *media res* to determine what crisis they are facing. Leaders using this handbook to prepare for a crisis in advance should think of past experiences or forecast potential disasters that may affect their organization.

While Chapters 5 through 8 will provide bespoke crisis leadership techniques, Chapter 4 will discuss leadership topics that are relevant regardless of crisis type.

CHAPTER **4**

Cross-case issues

The following *Crisis Leadership* chapters will further describe the unique approaches that should be taken for each crisis type, but there are some essential leadership skills that are relevant in *all* situations, regardless of category. Leaders must be able to communicate effectively, use public perception to their advantage, manage their own and their team's emotions, and be prepared for the crisis to change, escalate, and cross boundaries. Below is an initial exploration of these concepts.

COMMUNICATION

In a crisis, one of a leader's primary responsibilities is to impart and exchange information with their response teams, other organizations, and the public. Leaders should ensure that their team has the same understanding of the situation at all times. This can be done using a common operational perspective (COP). They must also share information rapidly and seamlessly, meaning that all crisis response teams, both internal and external, receive information in a timely manner. Leaders should also set clear expectations of their teams and be prepared to use an integrated command system (ICS) when multiple organizations are involved in the crisis response. All of these concepts will be explained further in the following sections.

COMMON OPERATIONAL PERSPECTIVES

Leaders are responsible for establishing a shared reality for their response teams, meaning that *all* responders, regardless of organization, operate under the same understanding of the situation with clearly expressed expectations.

DOI: 10.4324/9781003289180-4

When responders share the same understanding of the situation, they have the same perception of the situation, including what is taking place, where it is happening, and what the leaders' expectations are. Leaders can create this shared reality by developing a common operational perspective (COP).

A COP is a single display of relevant information shared by more than one emergency operations center to facilitate collaborative planning and information. COPs are crucial to sensemaking during a crisis. They enable members of the emergency operations center to make decisions and take unified action by allowing an entire response structure to work together in crisis resolution. They do this by collecting, clarifying, and disseminating key information.

> *"A common operational picture is established and maintained by the gathering, collating, synthesizing, and disseminating of incident information to all appropriate parties involved in an incident. Achieving a common operating picture allows on-scene and off-scene personnel to have the same information about the incident, including the availability and location of resources, personnel, and the status of requests for assistance."*
> – US National Incident Management System

Extreme crisis researchers debate whether COPs are products, processes, or operating environments.

- As a *product*, COPs often look like a geographical or visual representation of the crisis site and a checklist that describes the characteristics of the response. The COP is accessible—either located centrally or virtually—enabling all responders to refer to it at all times to inform their response and behavior.

  For example, an organization facing a cyberattack may draw a map of all affected servers and assign specific IT professionals to mitigate the risk at each site. This map and to-do list might be available in a central meeting place like the company headquarters or online as a shared document.

- As a *process*, developing a COP requires continuous conversation and clarification, while responders gather, synthesize, and disseminate information to all parties in a crisis response. This is updated as the crisis progresses, and the COP continues to evolve alongside the response.

For example, an organization facing a cyberattack may start to take note of all affected sites on a shared email chain. As more information is learned, a leader will send regular updates about what servers have been attacked already, which attacks have been mitigated, and which will be handled next.

- As an *operating environment*, COPs are methods of continuous sensemaking—they define the circumstances of the response and serve as a touchpoint for crisis responders to refer to as a description of the situation.

  For example, an organization facing a cyberattack may continue to generate understanding of a situation by having regular meetings with stakeholders and updating the definition of what has happened—what servers have been attacked, how many attacks have been mitigated, etc. This description of the crisis' status is available to all stakeholders at all times.

In a singular crisis response, COPs can be used as all three: A physical object (product), a method of working toward a goal (process), or a way of defining the situation (operating environment). All three characterizations of a COP are similar in that the goal is to create a shared understanding of the crisis. When synthesized and implemented, COPs can successfully mitigate confusion and chaos associated with extreme crisis response.

RAPID AND SEAMLESS COMMUNICATION

In coordination with a COP, leaders must create a system of information sharing that is both rapid and seamless. There must be infrastructure in place (e.g., walkie-talkies, cell phones, phone towers, etc.). If not, this must be established immediately.

For communications to be rapid, there must be a conveyance method that quickly transmits decisions and directives from high-level meetings down to the on-scene responders.

Seamless communications necessitate a clear directive of *what* can be shared with *whom*. Relationships must be made with internal and external press and communications departments to be strategically leveraged when necessary.

Once a system of rapid and seamless communication is established, it should be used to set response expectations clearly. This can include a shared understanding of terminology and an explicit division of responsibility, so that it is clear what must be done, when it should be done, and who must do it.

INCIDENT COMMAND SYSTEMS

When crises become more complex, many response organizations may become involved. This requires modification of communication strategies. Not every organization uses the same terminology, method, or frequency of information dissemination. Leaders must understand the differences between their own organizational communication strategies and those of other, partner organizations, as well as understand the situation as it exists on the ground. One way to do this is through an incident command system (ICS).

ICSs are widely applicable management systems designed to enable efficient crisis management by integrating facilities, personnel, equipment, communications, and response procedures by combining response organizations to act as one organization. ICS is a collection of standardized job titles, responsibilities, and terminology that sets clear expectations for roles and establishes common processes for planning and managing resources. This system has been mandated by the United States government for major response organizations to standardize organizational response *in situ*.

For example, a hospital system falls victim to a cyberattack that seeks to hold patient information for ransom. They must call on IT professionals, law enforcement, and government officials to assist in the mitigation of the attack and recovery of patient data, as well as legal and public relations teams to handle the media and communicate with affected stakeholders. They must act swiftly and join forces, using a pre-established ICS to designate a public information officer, liaison officer, operations team, and planning and logistic sections to help quickly and effectively set up an organization that is ready for action.

ICSs are designed to clarify tasks related to crisis response to dispel confusion that develops when multiple agencies work together during major disasters. It requires organizations to use common terminology and manage event response by tasks. In theory, it is scalable, flexible, and applicable to all crises regardless of size, complexity, and duration.

However, critics of ICSs argue that in reality it is cumbersome, slow, and inflexible, because ICSs force organizations to appoint team members to temporary positions that may not be relevant for the crisis at hand. An ICS becomes even more limited in extreme environments, where nimble response and action are necessary. The following chapters will highlight strategies to navigate using an ICS to an organization's advantage when responding to crises of varying severity.

SOCIAL AMPLIFICATION

Extreme crises do not occur in a vacuum, isolated from public view. Crisis leaders will often be the representatives for disasters, charged with framing the event for the public. However, leaders' ability to shape the narrative stops there. Not only does the public view crisis situations, but they also influence the response. Once the public better understands the event, they begin to—often inspired by media outlets—frame the issue in their own terms. The public's perspective might be manifested and influenced by mass media, social media, lawsuits, government intervention, or other social mechanisms. This effect is known as *social amplification*.

There is no comprehensive theory that explains why certain crises produce massive public reactions, especially when events with minor risks are perceived disproportionately by the public to be larger threats than they actually are. The *social amplification of risk* framework is a concept that attempts to explain this. It argues that social amplification consists of information flow from the event that feeds the amplification channels, and then the reaction either attenuates or amplifies risk perception; this begins the ripple effect.

Social amplification can cause ripple effects that may affect the response organization, its industry, or other groups involved in the crisis both directly and indirectly. Through this process, the public itself becomes a transmitter that can either moderate or heighten the consequences of the crisis. For example, during the coronavirus pandemic, public understanding of the efficacy of mask wearing impacted the rate at which the virus spread and thus the number of hospitalized cases and severity of the crisis. In this way, public understanding amplified both the consequences of the virus itself and the measures that the responders had to take.

FELT EMOTIONS

Emotions play a role in crisis management because they are unavoidable in the face of a disaster. Academic research discusses how emotions, especially supraliminal *felt* emotions (as opposed to emotions that exist subliminally, or under the surface), can be detrimental to cognitive thought, especially when leaders are evaluating or trying to understand a crisis. Felt emotions include fear, shame, guilt, embarrassment, anxiety, pride, or any other feeling that a responder may experience or express while confronting a crisis.

Felt emotions can cause significant alterations in normal leadership responses during an extreme event. Some researchers argue that felt emotion diminishes cognitive ability by drawing attention away from the task and toward an internal feeling of panic, leading to impulsive decisions. Negative emotions, such as shame or guilt, can have the strongest impact on decision-making. However, some felt emotions can also be helpful. Some research argues that felt emotions can actually facilitate sensemaking by sharpening the senses and increasing situational awareness.

A leader's ability to think is dependent on their awareness of the severity of a threat. When thoughts about a crisis are subliminal, the subconscious mind seeks positive emotions to offset these ideas and act as an antidote to fear. In an effort to self-soothe, the mind attempts to block out negative thoughts. Research shows that this helps the mind think more broadly and creatively.

However, once thinking about threats reaches supraliminal awareness, known as the "threshold effect," the mind narrows its focus. This can impact cognition significantly, with the mere thought of death limiting a leader's ability to think.

The continuum of felt emotions ranges from thoughts of success to worries about impending death. Organizations generally plan for routine events, so during these crises, responders' felt emotions are subliminally positive, with thoughts of eventual success. If an event surpasses the routine or the fathomable, then trust in leadership fades and feelings of skepticism toward the crisis response plan emerge. Up to Black Elephant crisis events, feelings of skepticism are generally subliminal. As the event severity progresses beyond the organization's ability to respond or expand their response, felt emotions of failure or death anxiety often transition from subliminal to supraliminal.

MORTALITY SALIENCE

A responder's awareness of impending death, also called *mortality salience*, correlates with that person's ability to think. As mortality salience increases, cognition decreases. Even if one has high cognitive abilities, they are not likely to suppress mortality salience.

As a result, people experiencing high mortality salience continue to think about death despite the presence of supraliminal positive emotions or thoughts. This means that leaders' positive reinforcement in dangerous contexts is not necessarily impactful. When faced with imminent death, moral judgments become clouded by the natural fight or flight instinct, so responders are tempted to act only in their own self-interest. When consumed by thoughts of death, people tend to lose focus on even the smallest of tasks, and this cognitive narrowing may prevent people from giving full cognitive attention to other conflicts. In these scenarios, leaders should focus on building trust with their teams and emphasizing the importance of nuanced tasks.

Mortality salience is one reason that COP and ICS are so important. These emergency response tools are a rational counterbalance to the felt emotions that can disrupt sensemaking and decision-making by leaders closest to the crisis.

RESPECT

At the core of any strong crisis response is a well-functioning team that supports one another's emotions and values their teammate's input and work. In addition to being aware of their teams' felt emotions, leaders should work to foster a respectful work environment. The key attributes of a respectful work environment are:

- **Respect is evident**—everyone is treated with dignity and respect.
- **Opinions are valued**—individuals are encouraged to voice concerns, provide suggestions, and raise questions. Differing opinions are respected.
- **There is a high level of trust**—trust is fostered among individuals and teams throughout the organization.
- **Conflict resolution is fair**—leaders use objective methods to resolve conflicts.

ESCALATION OF EVENTS

As discussed in the previous chapter, routine crises can escalate into extreme events. This escalation brings with it new considerations for crisis leadership and decision-making. As crises increase in severity, organizations will reach a *critical instability point* in which a situation transitions from one crisis type to another.

These transitions are important because they represent points where decision-making can become decentralized, and more leaders can be incorporated. Boundaries may become "fuzzy" as more actors become involved, bringing new perspectives, ideas, and methods of leadership. The direction an organization takes at this transition point is dependent upon the readiness of the organization to handle increasingly complex events.

The primary difference between a crisis and an *extreme* crisis is the increased complexity of decision-making. At the point where an event becomes an extreme crisis, actively preparing to take on leadership challenges should be front of mind.

One way that leaders can counteract escalation is by pre-establishing relationships with outside organizations that they may need to call on in case of a crisis. This means that before an event occurs, leaders should have an idea of organizations they may work with and determine hierarchies and methods of communication. Once a crisis occurs, this predetermined structure can provide a basis for an evolving system of management that adjusts to the situation at hand.

TRANSBOUNDARY CRISES

In an increasingly interconnected world, crises can surpass the physical locations where they occur. The more complex a crisis is, the more potential it has to affect multiple life-sustaining systems or infrastructures; these consequences are known as transboundary effects. For example, the 2008 financial crisis began in the United States but quickly escalated to a global situation due to multinational financial institutions and global banking practices. Typically, crises with transboundary effects are non-linear and cascade in seriousness.

> Transboundary crises:
> * Exist cross-functionally and cross-nationally
> * Have no defined beginning, end, or location
> * Escalate quickly in unforeseen directions
> * Cause unfathomable damage

The reason that transboundary crises can be so damaging is that organizations struggle to keep pace with this challenging and changing environment.

The tactics that leaders can use to mitigate transboundary crises are riddled with complications but serve as good first steps.

To combat transboundary crises, leaders should:

- Prepare for a crisis that others may not want to take on or recognize as legitimate
- Try to make sense of an emerging and evolving crisis
- Manage large response networks
- Learn under pressure

Because transboundary crises often happen in the abstract, they do not have one responsible party that must lead the crisis response. Therefore, leaders should prepare to take on a crisis that other involved stakeholders may not want to take on or recognize as legitimate. They must also try and make sense of this crisis as it emerges and evolves, practicing continued sensemaking and actively trying to understand the situation. They must manage larger response networks than are required for other crises, incorporating other response organizations. Strong leaders will also continue to learn under pressure, not allowing rigid or known strategies to prevent effective leadership.

Leaders facing a transboundary crisis must consider that unconventional situations might require unconventional solutions. Leaders should remain open-minded to innovative, even develop "clumsy," solutions. Creativity in crisis response can seem antithetical to the normal operations of prepared organizations that often derive certainty from well-established procedures. Nevertheless, creativity is an invaluable leadership tool when responding to such complex crises.

Chapters 5 to 8 will provide more specific leadership advice, categorized by crisis type and increasing in severity, from Black Elephant to Black Swan crises.

CHAPTER **5**

Black Elephant crises

- **Situational context:** Black Elephant crises come as a *surprise* to responders. Even though information is known and the consequences to responders and their communities are low, emergency operations centers have never faced this type of crisis before.
- **Sensemaking:** Leaders can make sense of a Black Elephant crisis by *updating* or adjusting and correcting mental models as new information is learned about the event. They should be sure to do this calmly.
- **Decision-making:** Responders can determine how to best resolve the crisis using *recognition primed* decision-making or applying past experiences to the current situation.
- **Crisis response:** Encouraging *cooperative* teamwork among existing groups in the emergency operations center can help organizations expand their ability to respond to surprise crises. This means having typically separate teams work together toward crisis resolution.
- **Leadership:** Leaders should be prepared to *adapt* their routine/typical leadership to a new situation. They should focus on listening, respecting, and connecting with their teams.

DOI: 10.4324/9781003289180-5

SITUATIONAL CONTEXT

Leaders are faced with many potential crises and must decide which to actively prevent, which to simply mitigate, and which to ignore. However, just because a hazard is ignored does not mean that it is risk-free. When predictable hazards escalate, as they often do, and combine with organizational vulnerabilities, leaders can be faced with a *surprise crisis*. Leaders are aware of the potential for these events and may implement measures to offset their consequences. But mitigative actions do not fully eliminate the chance for a surprise crisis to occur. So why don't organizations actively prevent these surprises? Leaders often become satisfied with mere mitigation because elimination of the problem before it becomes a crisis is too complex or costly. Thus, surprises lurk, their consequences building as a potential crisis looms.

Key traits:

- *Information* about the event is **known**
- The event's *consequences* are **moderate**
- The prior *action* taken is to **mitigate**

Investor and environmentalist, Adam Sweidan, coined the term *Black Elephant* to describe such surprise crises. Sweidan illustrated the phrase with two current examples: Climate change and freshwater pollution. These issues are widely recognized as potentially dangerous (e.g., climate change leading to increasing global temperatures and freshwater pollution limiting natural resources), and strategies can be employed to limit their consequences (e.g., limitation of carbon emissions and recycling efforts).

While these efforts do not fully mitigate the potential for an eventual crisis, leaders are discouraged from solving the underlying/actual issue because it would be too complex or costly to do so (e.g., ending the use of fossil fuels and investing in renewable energy). However, these mitigation strategies can be rendered inefficient in the face of situational changes the equivalent of the Elephant charging in. Situational changes (e.g., the start of a wildfire or an oil spill) can signal the arrival of the much-feared Black Elephant crisis.

There are herds of Black Elephants out there, many of whom are not actively causing problems. The challenge arises when a Black Elephant unexpectedly rears its head to cause a crisis. Its appearance comes as a surprise because, until then, mitigation efforts appeared to be working. Black Elephant crises cause chaos in the routine response strategies. This chaos is a result of insufficient training, experience, policies, or strategies. By the time the Elephant has arrived, it is too late—in the midst of the crisis is not the time to develop these attributes.

Black Elephants are more unpredictable than routine, or White Swan crises, which crisis response teams tackle regularly using a practiced response plan. They differ from Gray Rhino crises, covered in Chapter 6, in that leaders do take some steps to mitigate the effects of Black Elephant crises before they occur.

Case study

Apollo 13 as a Black Elephant crisis

 On April 11, 1970, Apollo 13, a spacecraft carrying three NASA astronauts left the Kennedy Space Center in Houston, Texas, and launched toward the moon. Two days into its journey, a routine stir of an oxygen tank ignited a damaged wire and dispelled Apollo 13's oxygen supply into space. NASA had planned for many "normal," or expected disruptions but they had not planned for this specific contingency.

Despite a lack of preparedness—the spacecraft was only designed to support two men on the moon for two days—mission control in Houston improvised new procedures to support more astronauts for longer, splashing down safely on Earth days later. NASA leaders avoided catastrophe by tackling the Black Elephant with appropriate sensemaking, decision-making, crisis response, and leadership skills.

The Apollo 13 crisis was not a Gray or Black Swan crisis because NASA understood the cause of the explosion but were faced with new challenges of repairing onboard systems and making course corrections to get the crew back to Earth safely. NASA had the experience and capability to resolve the crisis (a Gray or Black Swan occurs when the crisis extends beyond the organization's capacity). Also, the type of crisis depends on its scale of consequence. The Apollo 13 crisis, while dangerous for the astronauts, was mainly a reputational crisis; NASA could recover its reputation. The lives of the NASA leadership and the wider community were not in jeopardy; thus, it was not a catastrophic crisis.

SENSEMAKING

Leaders must release their rigid, routine response mindsets and be prepared to adapt to surprise crises. For Black Elephant crises, sensemaking means constantly developing a flexible understanding of the situation. This often involves non-linear thinking, and the responders' acquired knowledge and intuition, to develop a common perspective of the crisis, make good decisions, and act their way into novel solutions. Responders in a Black Elephant crisis can build on their sensemaking abilities by *updating*.

Updating means refining the understanding of events by adjusting and correcting mental models as new information is learned. Leaders should always be appropriately skeptical of the information presented to them, and all interpretations of events or courses of action should be changeable/evolving. Essentially, leaders should be prepared to rethink their understanding of the crisis and how they should act *while* they respond.

> Sensemaking for a Black Elephant crisis involves a dynamic understanding of the situation by updating mental models.

The crisis may happen suddenly, like the explosion aboard Apollo 13, but while the response must be immediate, it will likely require a more complex, long-term solution. Sensemaking for a Black Elephant crisis involves a dynamic understanding of the situation by updating mental models throughout the duration of the response.

Updated thinking requires responders to reject their previous mindset of a straightforward event (e.g., landing safely on the moon) and to embrace disorder (e.g., repairing vital systems while adjusting the spaceship's course). To update their mental models throughout the response, leaders must continue to establish a clear picture of the situation through consistent communication and information gathering.

Information gathering might look like talking to on-scene actors about what they are experiencing or talking to technical experts who are interpreting data from the event. For example, mission control talked directly to and frequently with astronauts aboard Apollo 13 throughout their response and synthesized this information with mission control's data to create a shared understanding of the situation; this formed the basis for decision-making and crisis response activity.

Felt emotions

Crisis leaders must do all of this—actively understand the situation by communicating and gathering data—calmly. In Black Elephant crises, the situation exceeds what has been prepared for but does not exceed what the organization can manage. Responders should react to surprises with confidence in the knowledge that their organization can in fact manage the crisis to prevent escalation. One of the most pertinent characteristics of a Black Elephant crisis is that the felt emotions of the responder begin to influence the responders' ability to lead, make sense of the crisis, and make effective decisions. When experiencing emotions, such as a fear of failure or doubt about the organization's ability to mitigate the crisis, the responder's focus on logistical response considerations begins to take a lower priority.

> When felt emotions begin to influence the crisis response, responders should briefly step back and refocus on a singular goal.

Surprise itself is a strong enough emotion to throw responders off—generating fear and doubt in their capabilities. When felt emotions inevitably begin to influence the crisis response, responders should briefly step back so that they can better understand the conditions in which they must make decisions. In a Black Elephant crisis, this can be done by setting a singular goal.

For example, after the explosion, Apollo 13's mission control director set the primary objective of their mission as getting astronauts back to Earth alive. This focused aim allowed for refocusing and prevented chaos among the team. The key to setting a priority is to make it a *bigger-picture objective*, not a *method* of getting to the goal. For example, the mission control director did not make the primary aim restoring systems inside of the space shuttle, but rather the safe return of the astronauts. If leaders focus on methods rather than objectives, they might become trapped in a linear response and be more disrupted by setbacks and therefore less effective in resolving the crisis.

DECISION-MAKING

For Black Elephants, routine crisis decision-making processes may be insufficient, but leaders still have the experience and capability to adapt. Responders can modify their status quo decision-making processes to better fit Black Elephant crises.

Theoretical background: Recognition primed decision-making

The theory of *recognition primed* decision[1]-making suggests that prior experience helps decision-making processes so that when Black Elephant crises appear, leaders are better able to use their experience to adapt normal procedures to the situation at hand. Recognition primed decision-making identifies three essential attributes for effective decision-making, *experience*, *intuition*, and *instinct*:

- **Experience** is the leader's past training and encounters with similar crisis situations.
- **Intuition** is the leader's ability to make decisions instinctively, and without much reasoning.
- **Instinct** is the combination of experience and intuition—the leader's innate response to certain stimuli.

These attributes can be developed prior to Black Elephant crises to better prepare a leader to respond. Experience is gained from repeated drilling and procedural training, while intuition can be tested by gauging a leader's response. Improved instincts will be the result of this regular training and assessment. For example, the Apollo 13 crew spent over 400 hours in flight simulators and flight controllers participated in emergency simulations prior to lift-off. Though there was no exact contingency plan in place, the astronauts and responders were able to expand on their experience to improvise crisis resolution for the explosion and oxygen depletion.

Effective crisis responders make decisions with limited information and data in times of uncertainty. Recognition primed decision-making suggests three processes that can help responders do this when facing Black Elephant crisis, *simple match*, *situation diagnosis*, *evaluation*:

- **Simple match** occurs when the responder recognizes a similar crisis from their past experience and directly associates its response to the current crisis.

  For example, a mission control team has also worked on a spacecraft that experienced an explosion and lost oxygen and can transfer those learnings exactly to the Apollo 13 mission.
- **Situation diagnosis** occurs when relevant clues from the current crisis are compared with several past crises, and the leader selects, adapts, and implements known responses.

  For example, a mission control team has worked on a spacecraft that experienced an explosion and on a different spacecraft that needed to quickly change course. The responders combine those experiences to respond to the Apollo 13 disaster.

- **Evaluation** occurs when a responder develops an entirely novel solution and course of action which they then assess to integrate past experiences and actions into the crisis at hand.

  For example, a mission control team rehearsed what might happen if an engine was lost mid-flight. When Apollo 13 experiences an explosion and must return to Earth, the team creates an entirely new solution but compares the response to the practiced engine-loss plan, incorporating similar response protocols and ensuring attention to detail.

Practical advice: How to make decisions in a Black Elephant crisis

Crisis decision-making requires leaders to think quickly (Chapter 4, Cross-Case Issues highlights the need to match decision-making speed with the rate of crisis escalation). While responding *in situ*, responders must also predict the future course of the crisis to prepare the organization for what might come. Responders must outpace the crisis, which requires preparing for all potential outcomes.

Responders make decisions in dynamic, uncertain, and time-pressured situations by recognizing previous and similar crises. They should use their previous experience to see clues in the new situation and implement previously used strategies, or, if responders are lacking in experience, they should take time to learn about historical crises or practice emergency situations. Researchers generally agree that both formal and informal continuous and periodic education and training that stresses adaptive management to help cope with crises and disasters help responders make sense of crisis situations and react appropriately. For example, a new NASA trainee may study past space shuttle disasters and how they were responded to before starting in the mission control center.

In Black Elephant crisis response, responders may use cognitive heuristics, or "rules of thumb," that enable leaders to make fast decisions that are "good enough," or sufficient to deescalate the situation to the status quo. Relying on mental shortcuts can reduce the cognitive load that leaders face. For example, if a NASA scientist knows that the first step to respond to a crisis is to report it to the mission controller, they can do this without much thought and begin the crisis response more smoothly.

Leaders may use their metacognition skills to enable experienced responders to recognize, critique, and correct their decisions while executing their proposed course of action. This may involve making tradeoffs between normal organization operation and practical response actions, meaning leaders may need to break some rules to resolve the crisis. For example, NASA typically required material of a certain standard to be used externally on spacecrafts. However, the Apollo 13 crisis superseded usual protocol, and astronauts worked with responders to repurpose on-board material to plug the hole and prevent rising CO_2.

There are some important considerations as leaders make decisions in the emergency operations center. Leaders should:

- Change perspectives when needed (understand both the big picture and the smaller details of the crisis)
- Think about and plan for the worst-case scenario
- Identify potential blind spots and areas of uncertainty
- Recognize the organization's limits, know when to call for outside help
- Manage organizational risks and technical risks
- Clarify the chain of command and identify the decision maker(s)

For leaders to change perspectives when needed, they must think about the bigger picture while making on-the-ground decisions. They can do this by setting a larger goal, as outlined in the *Sensemaking* section above, and communicating with people involved in the crisis response. Leaders should regularly toggle between the two perspectives and use both to inform one another. For example, mission control might speak to astronauts aboard Apollo 13 about which systems have shut down. However, if they do this while maintaining an understanding that the goal is to return the astronauts to Earth, they may prioritize recovering systems for touchdown rather than systems that were relevant for the intended moon landing.

Along with the bigger picture, responders must prepare for a worst-case scenario as the situation unfolds. One way to do this is to identify potential blind spots and areas of uncertainty and forecast what might happen if all response efforts fail. Leaders can identify blind spots by thinking about what information they might need to know for a successful result and what they do not yet know or will be unable to know. In this process, they can begin to gather information about and prepare for a worst-case scenario. For example, while mission control during the Apollo 13 mission was focused on landing the astronauts safely on Earth, they had to prepare for the potential that the shuttle would not return and consider what factors might make that a possibility, such as being unable to plug the hole leaking oxygen.

Leaders also must manage the organizational and technical risks, including clarifying the chain of command and identifying who must make decisions. This is where common operational perspective (COP) and integrated command system (ICS) systems can be relied on (see Chapter 4 for more information). For example, there was a clear leadership structure and division of responsibility among Apollo 13's mission control: Only one member could communicate with the astronauts and project managers were assigned to mitigate the various hazards on board.

CRISIS RESPONSE

Because Black Elephants are routine crises, teams already have a frame of reference on how to respond. They must expand these capabilities through increased cooperation to meet the surprise crisis' demands. Once the Black Elephant crisis has been recognized, leaders can use surprise management response strategies which require responders to reject stability and equilibrium to adapt to the demands of the crisis. This means managing the event at the threshold where the situation appears stable but is on the verge of chaos, what academic literature calls *creative breakdown*.

In crisis leadership, creative breakdowns, or disruptions to the established response, create an opportunity to expand crisis response capabilities through *cooperation*. The chaos created by the breakdown forces teams to engage in new methods of teamwork. During a Black Elephant crisis, leaders *act* their way into new capabilities, meaning they create new solutions simply by working together to do what needs to be done.

There are some important considerations as leaders in emergency operations centers respond to the crisis. Leaders should:

- Recognize that teams are stronger together than the sum of their parts
- Adopt a test-and-learn approach
- Remain focused on a common goal

Leaders' role here is to recognize that teams are stronger together than the sum of their individual parts. Collaborative crisis response brings together the various parts of an emergency operation center to work toward a common goal. Teams should take responsibility over their specialized areas and come together to discuss potential solutions and responses. For example, NASA called on its engineers, material scientists, and logistics teams to work on ways to bring the astronauts home safely.

A test-and-learn approach can help teams respond to a Black Elephant crisis. This means that teams act and then evaluate whether or not these steps have worked toward mitigating the crisis. To do this, teams must keep an open mind and be willing to accept when a tested response fails. For example, mission control tried and tested a number of methods to control the disappearing oxygen. Each potential solution was interrogated and evaluated before being recommended to the team in space.

Again, remaining steadfastly focused on a common goal can help teams generate a cultural drive that rejects failure. For example, leaders at NASA focused solely on returning the astronauts to Earth. This goal drove the crisis response at every level, preventing teams from giving up on their individual assignments because a larger success was at stake.

In sum, a Black Elephant crisis response should be collaborative, with responders keeping an open mind to potential solutions and acting their way into new possibilities.

LEADERSHIP

During a Black Elephant crisis, leaders must *adapt* their routine leadership styles to the situation's demands. In this crisis, leaders might be drawn out of the familiar and into uncharted territory. Leadership adaptations consist of both improvisation and ambidextrous styles—they must be able to think on their feet to determine what exploration and work their teams should do.

To foster strong team relationships, leaders should:

- Listen to their teams
- Show respect for their teams and the work that they are doing
- Connect with other responders as much as possible

While leaders will of course give commands during a crisis response, they should foster a strong relationship with their teams. This means they listen to, respect, and connect with their teams. This means taking the teams' suggestions into consideration and evaluating when responders need to rest or need encouragement. For example, Apollo 13's mission control commander was able to trust his team of technically proficient experts entirely to formulate an effective response; he primarily guided and streamlined their ideas and work. He connected with his team by staying "in the trenches" with them, working alongside the rest of mission control for the duration of the response.

To generate an effective crisis response, leaders should:

- Seek to align responders to their training, procedures, and experience quickly
- Ensure their own calmness and readiness to lead
- Maintain a positive attitude despite information gaps
- Develop a battle rhythm that promotes strong communication throughout the response organization
- Develop a COP so that what is being communicated is consistent and clear
- Establish a collaborative decision-making process early in the crisis
- Adapt past experiences to the current challenges (recognition primed decision-making)

Once in the midst of a Black Elephant crisis, leaders must use their experience to devise effective solutions. Leaders should return the responders to the familiar quickly so that the crisis can be mitigated using experience and traditional protocol. This is accomplished by remaining calm and stretching their own experience to meet new challenges.

In any crisis, leaders should be aware of their own emotions. Black Elephant crises will make leaders uncomfortable, and they may start to feel worried or afraid. Effective leadership includes adapting to these uncomfortable emotions and returning as quickly as possible to calmness. Leaders must monitor their physical and emotional state to ensure that they retain the ability to direct others throughout the crisis; this includes the ability to listen, show respect, and connect with other responders.

Maintaining a positive attitude about information shortages helps drive the motivation of the emergency operations center. To calm themselves and effectively mitigate the Black Elephant, leaders must continue to acquire new knowledge of the situation. During a Black Elephant crisis, there will be gaps in information and data flow, but they should not be large enough to make the event unfathomable. Responders and leaders must maintain a positive mindset about any information gaps to return the organization to familiar crisis response protocols as quickly as possible.

Leaders should develop a battle rhythm that promotes strong communication throughout the response organization. Leaders are charged with setting a response pace that keeps teams on-task and working together. This pace should be quick enough to keep the response ahead of the crisis but disciplined enough to be sustainable should the crisis continue for a long period of time. When setting the battle rhythm and responding, leaders should consider the capabilities of the organization (i.e., *What can be handled on-site? Do other response teams need to be called in for support?*).

Common operational perspectives are useful in establishing a shared reality. Leaders can call on this tool during a Black Elephant to help reduce chaos and center the response. Because a Black Elephant crisis is just outside of a routine crisis response, leaders might be able to adapt standard response protocols to develop the COP. For example, during the Apollo 13 crisis response, mission control revised their existing to-do lists to meet the demands of the disaster.

Leaders should establish a collaborative decision-making process early in the crisis. This means incorporating teamwork into the response and using all capabilities offered by the emergency response organization. Typically for a Black Elephant crisis, this looks like expanding traditional roles to meet more advanced challenges. For example, the NASA engineers who designed the space shuttle with traditional materials had to learn more about the supplies onboard to create an impromptu hole covering and stop the oxygen leak.

Sometimes leadership adaptation involves an expansion of existing organizational capacity and sometimes it involves adding expertise or knowledge to the crisis. This calls on recognition primed decision-making skills like experience, intuition, and instinct (discussed earlier in the *Decision-Making* section).

In Black Elephant crises, the solutions are usually within reach. However, implementing the solutions might involve expanding leadership or organizational capacity using the techniques described above to match the demands of the crisis.

Although some information is known about the event before it occurs, Black Elephant crises come as a surprise to responders. To make sense of the situation, responders must update their mental models and understanding of the situation. To make decisions, responders can apply past experiences to the current situation, using recognition primed decision-making. Their organizations are not fully prepared to take on the crisis and must expand their capabilities through cooperative teamwork to respond to the crisis. Leaders should be prepared to adapt their typical leadership style to this new situation, with a focus on listening to and connecting with their teams.

While the above strategies should equip leaders to handle Black Elephant crises, sometimes leaders are less prepared to take on a crisis situation. In this case, leaders fail to address vulnerabilities before they combine with hazards to become Gray Rhino crises. These will be explored in the next chapter.

NOTE

1 Bond, S., & Cooper, S. (2006). Modeling emergency decisions: recognition-primed decision making. The literature in relation to an ophthalmic critical incident. Journal of clinical nursing, 15(8). Klein, G. (1998) Sources of Power: How People Make Decisions, MIT Press, Cambridge, Mass, pp. 1-30.

CHAPTER 6

Gray Rhino crises

- **Situational context:** Gray Rhino crises occur when responders *fail* to mitigate obvious hazards before they threaten organizational weaknesses. Even though information is known and the consequences to responders and their communities are potentially very high, emergency operations centers reason why *not* to act on a problem instead of taking preventative steps.
- **Sensemaking:** Leaders can use *enacted* sensemaking to understand a Gray Rhino crisis. This means that responders begin to understand their situation by taking (even small) action(s) to resolve it.
- **Decision-making:** Responders can determine how to best resolve the crisis using *macrocognition* decision-making or applying data and previous experiences to continuously inform the current situation.
- **Crisis response:** New methods of *complex* teamwork among the emergency operations center and external organizations groups can help organizations expand their ability to respond to failure crises. This means having different groups work on different tasks simultaneously to reach a common goal.
- **Leadership:** Leaders should be prepared to use *nonlinear* leadership techniques that rely on understanding the evolving situation by asking questions and learning from those around them rather than relying on their typical crisis response strategies. They should focus on listening, respecting, and connecting with their teams.

DOI: 10.4324/9781003289180-6

SITUATIONAL CONTEXT

Potential disasters loom for almost all organizations and though some hazards will inevitably combine with organizational weaknesses to cause a crisis, leaders sometimes choose not to take any mitigating action. These crises have high consequences, but they are often neglected because of their size and, paradoxically, their likelihood; the problem just seems too big or too complex to solve in advance. When faced with such crises, it is easier for leaders to *muddle*, or reason why *not* to act on a problem, than it is to take steps to mitigate, or prevent a crisis. This *failure* to act on a foreseeable and highly probable crisis leads to worsened consequences when disaster does inevitably strike.

Key traits:

- *Information* about the event is **known**
- The event's *consequences* are **high**
- The prior *action* taken is to **muddle**

Author and political analyst, Michele Wucker, coined the term *Gray Rhino* to describe such crises. These disasters are harder to ignore, but are neglected, nonetheless. They may either be a distance away, providing organizations a chance to prepare, or they may already be charging toward the response organization. Regardless, when a Gray Rhino rears its head, the crisis is a result of inaction on the leaders' behalf. The sooner leaders accept that the Rhino is charging toward them they can begin to act.

One purpose of this chapter is to encourage leaders to look for Gray Rhino crises they might be facing earlier so that they can prepare for, and hopefully sidestep, a stampede. It can also be used by leaders who are facing a Gray Rhino crisis now and do not want to be trampled.

There are different types of Gray Rhinos. They can come one at a time or many can approach together in a "clash." They can arrive slowly or charge quickly ahead. Either way, they threaten to flatten whatever stands in their path and early identification is key to mitigating their damage; failure to do so creates a crisis situation.

There are four types of Gray Rhinos that might cause crises: *Charging, recurring, meta,* and *unidentified.* The following descriptions include examples of emergency operation centers handling these rhinos:

- **Charging Rhinos** must be dealt with *right away.* These crises are imminent; leaders should determine how quickly they are approaching and how much damage they are going to do. Then, they can begin to plan a response.

  For example, a hurricane is growing in size and approaching an urban center rapidly. In the days leading up to the storm, leaders must determine how much potential damage the storm will cause to decide whether or not citizens should be evacuated.

- **Recurring Rhinos** have happened before. Leaders have some kind of roadmap for how to handle these, but it may need to be modified regularly. The best way to approach a recurring rhino is to take preventative measures.

  For example, the flu virus strikes every year with a new, slightly different strain. Medical organizations like the CDC actively prepare variations of the flu vaccine to counter it.

- **Meta Rhinos** can be the most dangerous. These are structural factors that hinder an organization's ability to respond to a crisis. Meta Rhinos are often homogenous teams whose shared backgrounds and demographics limit diverse perspectives on potential crises and solutions.

  For example, a car company's leadership knows that the car has a faulty ignition switch which could threaten lives. However, the company culture is homogeneous, prioritizing profits over consumer safety. So, the company is slow to recall the vehicles.

- **Unidentified Rhinos** are further away. These are looming crises with yet unclear threats. The nature of the challenge will become more visible as the threat approaches; so, the best thing for leaders to do in this scenario is to closely monitor the Rhino until an actionable challenge has arisen.

  For example, leaders in the technological space know that there will be potential crises associated with artificial intelligence; however, it is unclear what these will be just yet.

Once leaders identify which situation they are in, that is, which Gray Rhino they must take on, they can begin to act. Effective crisis responders see a Rhino for what it is and act as soon as possible.

The hazards that form Gray Rhino crises are harder to ignore than those that precede Black Elephant crises. The latter looms quietly and threatens only moderate consequences. Gray Rhinos, on the other hand, stomp and butt their heads, threatening disaster at a moment's notice. However, as opposed to more extreme crises, leaders still have the opportunity to act *before* these disasters strike because information about the event is known in advance.

CASE STUDY

Superstorm Sandy as a Gray Rhino crisis

On October 22, 2012, a tropical sea depression formed in the Caribbean Sea. Two days later, it moved northeast, strengthening into a hurricane as its path crossed over Haiti, Puerto Rico, and Cuba. It weakened upon reaching the Bahamas on October 27, 2012, but then reformed and moved toward the Northeastern United States (US)—an unusual weather event driven by warm waters. With a 1,000-mile radius, Superstorm Sandy progressed up the East Coast of the US, and unleashed havoc on New Jersey and New York, paralyzing the subway system, leaving over 8 million people without power, ruining hundreds of thousands of homes, and killing hundreds of people.

The high level of damage from Superstorm Sandy is attributed to a lack of preparedness; the US National Weather Service's models did not predict that the storm would affect the American Northeast. Additionally, despite rising global temperatures and their proximity to the Atlantic, New York City and New Jersey had no hurricane disaster plans and their flood wall infrastructure was out-of-date. As the storm became stronger, the National Hurricane Center issued warnings to leave, but it was too late—many individuals in Sandy's path were unable to evacuate.

Hurricane Sandy was more extreme than a Black Elephant crisis because the consequences were high: Human life, homes, and crucial infrastructure were at stake. Leaders were aware of the potential for a catastrophic weather event as global warming has increased the number of superstorms along the East Coast. However, they did not take preventative action, muddling through a solution to the impending crisis and, once the storm struck, failing to evacuate citizens in time. This was not a Gray or Black Swan, however, because information about the storm was known in advance of the crisis.

SENSEMAKING

Leaders facing a Gray Rhino will encounter sensemaking challenges throughout the response process. Gray Rhinos are *not* information starved, so knowledge about the situation (i.e., data) should be available. What leaders must determine is *how* to respond, and they do so through enacted sensemaking.

Enacted sensemaking means that crisis responders begin to understand the context of their situation by acting. These do not need to be big, complex actions, but rather small, simple tasks that work toward mitigating the crisis. Enacted sensemaking follows the logic that taking even small steps can clarify what the solution may be.

For example, while American weather models predicted that Hurricane Sandy would harmlessly spin out into the Atlantic Ocean, eight days before Sandy struck, the European Centre for Medium-Range Weather Forecasts (ECMRWF) predicted that the superstorm would hit the US. In order to clarify and better understand the situation, the US National Weather Service took the European model into consideration, re-running calculations and evaluating its validity, before confirming Sandy's path just four days prior to landfall. In this way, the small actions of consulting other teams and engaging with the data allowed leaders to come into a greater understanding of what they were facing and how to respond.

FELT EMOTIONS

Gray Rhinos are unique not only in the extent to which leaders are likely to ignore them, but also in the extent that this ignorance can enhance felt emotions and disrupt the crisis response. Responders' emotional reaction to Gray Rhinos typically follows this framework:

Denial—responders do not believe that there is a threat, so there is no need to act.

Muddling—responders have acknowledged the threat but can still reason their way out of acting.

Diagnosis—responders can no longer ignore the threat and switch to active planning.

Panic—responders experience frenzied anxiety in the face of an imminent crisis. In this stage, leaders are the most likely to act, but also the most likely to make mistakes.

Action—responders take intentional steps to avert the problem, including inspiring other organizations/actors to join in the efforts and adjusting their response strategies as needed.

The sooner that emergency operations centers can move out of denial and into action, the quicker the crisis can be resolved. Responders will naturally move through this framework over time as the crisis evolves, and while leaders should have patience with their teams as their emotions adjust to the realities of the situation, there are ways to quickly advance to action.

One way to swiftly move from *denial* to *action* is to be aware of each stage as it occurs and preempt the subsequent stage:

- If responders are aware that teams are in *denial* of a threat, they may start to *muddle* by suggesting action.
    - For example, after realizing that Hurricane Sandy was headed toward the US, European meteorologists might reach out to the National Weather Service and suggest reevaluating the American weather model.
- If teams are *muddling*, leaders may start to *diagnose* by describing the situation and planning a response.
    - For example, one day before Hurricane Sandy made landfall in the US and leaders were simply discussing what action to take, President Barack Obama signed an emergency declaration that allowed local governments to request federal aid to act on additional storm preparations.
- If teams are stuck *diagnosing* the issue rather than *acting*, leaders should take a small mitigative action—the smaller the action, the less likely teams are to panic.
    - For example, in the days leading up to Hurricane Sandy, the US government issued travel alerts in the Northeast. These alerts were recommendations not to travel, but they were not mandated travel bans, so they acted only to diagnose the severity of the impending storm. In response, leadership at Amtrak took small steps to prevent potentially dangerous travel, canceling some of their scheduled railway journeys in preparation for the storm.

Panic in the face of a Gray Rhino crisis is nearly inevitable, and leaders should be acutely aware that responders will panic before they can take measured action. One way leaders can distinguish between panic and action stages is by determining how much information was used to inform potential decisions and whether other actors are involved. Decisions made while panicking will be rushed and therefore ill-informed. Panicked decisions are also typically taken on-site and do not involve other actors and organizations.

Actors are likely in the action stage if their approach is logically informed and includes other parties. For example, decisions to put the National Guard and US Air Force on duty in the seven states threatened by Sandy both incorporated data about the hurricane's path and utilized the capabilities of external organizations.

DECISION-MAKING

When a Gray Rhino charges forward, taking any action at all is better than neglect. Even "wrong" decisions, influenced by anxiety or panic, can provide useful feedback that informs the response. Decision-making in Gray Rhino crises should be rooted in the information that is already known to or is generated by emergency operations centers. There will be data about the event available, and the key to an effective response is to both recognize and use it.

Theoretical background: Macrocognition decision-making

Leaders should use a *macrocognition*[1] decision-making process in which data is linked to the framing of the situation. This is a derivative of recognition primed decision-making discussed in Chapter 5 but builds on it by encouraging responders to use current and new data in addition to data from past experiences. Using this process, decision makers continue to update, reject, and replace thoughts to build their mental model of the situation while using past experiences and data collection to inform their current decisions. This will require an iterative channeling of information into the decision-making process and reevaluation of whether past decisions have mitigated or exacerbated the crisis. Macrocognition decision-making in response to a Gray Rhino should be data-based and evolving.

For example, emergency operation centers had to draw from meteorologists' data about storm severity as Hurricane Sandy moved up the coast to decide whether or not they should mandate massive urban evacuations. When the storm briefly weakened, the data did not suggest an evacuation was necessary. However, responders using macrocognition decision-making continued to update their model of the situation by comparing Sandy's weather signals to past hurricanes' and were able to detect when the hurricane's severity would necessitate an evacuation.

When situations are dynamic, uncertain, and time-pressured, responders must make decisions by recognizing previous and similar crises. They should use their previous experience to see clues in the new situation and implement previously used strategies. For example, a hurricane crisis responder may refer to strategies used in the Hurricane Katrina response before assisting in Hurricane Sandy relief.

Researchers generally agree that both formal and informal continuous and periodic education and training that stresses adaptive management to help cope with crises and disasters help responders make sense of crisis situations and react appropriately. For extreme storm management, this might look like hurricane drills in schools or practiced evacuations.

Practical advice: How to make decisions in a Gray Rhino crisis

In Gray Rhino responses, leaders may use their metacognition skills to enable experienced responders to recognize, critique, and correct their decisions while executing their proposed course of action. This may involve making tradeoffs between normal organization operation and practical response actions, meaning leaders may need to break some rules to resolve the crisis. For example, when citizens refused to evacuate during Hurricane Sandy, the National Weather Service used their warning system to emit the unusually pointed message to facilitate the response: "THINK ABOUT THE RESCUE/RECOVERY TEAMS WHO WILL RESCUE YOU IF YOU ARE INJURED OR RECOVER YOUR REMAINS IF YOU DO NOT SURVIVE."

There are some important considerations as leaders make decisions in the emergency operations center. Leaders should:
- Change perspectives when needed (understand both the big picture and the smaller details of the crisis)
- Think about and plan for the worst-case scenario
- Identify potential blind spots and areas of uncertainty
- Recognize the organization's limits and know when to call for outside help
- Manage organizational risks and technical risks
- Clarify the chain of command and identify the decision maker(s)

For leaders to change perspectives when needed, they must think about the bigger picture while making on-the-ground decisions. They can do this by routinely assessing data, as outlined in the section above, and communicating with people involved in the crisis response. Leaders should regularly toggle between the two perspectives and use both to inform one another. For example, the governor of New Jersey might speak to the National Weather Service to receive updates on the status of Hurricane Sandy and speak to the Coast Guard to receive updates on how many citizens have evacuated the beach.

He might use information about the storm to inform the Coast Guard's strategy for evacuation and use information about civilian evacuation status to generate a bigger-picture idea of the potential consequences of this superstorm.

Along with the bigger picture, responders must prepare for a worst-case scenario as the situation unfolds. One way to do this is to identify potential blind spots and areas of uncertainty and forecast what might happen if all response efforts fail. Leaders can identify blind spots by thinking about what information they might need to know and what they do not or cannot know. In this process, they can begin to gather information about and prepare for a worst-case scenario. For example, the Governor may not know how many civilians have refused to evacuate. This blind spot can inform action (take stronger measures to encourage evacuation) or understanding of consequences (potential casualties if no one else evacuates).

Leaders must also manage the organizational and technical risks, including clarifying the chain of command and identifying who must make decisions. This is where common operational perspective (COP) and integrated command system (ICS) systems can be relied on (see Chapter 4 for more information). For example, Hurricane Sandy covered a large region and required the incorporation of many emergency operation centers in its response. Once the President authorized federal support, the Federal Emergency Management Agency (FEMA) took charge and coordinated state and local governments, nongovernmental organizations, and tribal groups into an ICS, acting as the primary designator of roles and responsibilities.

CRISIS RESPONSE

Once a Gray Rhino crisis has been recognized, understood, and decisions have been made about its resolution, the crisis response becomes a rubric of *complex* processes. Many emergency operation centers must work separately toward one common goal: Mitigation. These complex processes often move toward the edge of chaos and become non-linear, even when ICSs and COPs are employed to reduce chaos.

With so many moving parts, leaders should be aware of cognitive biases that can impact the crisis response. Recognizing these potential biases both in teams and in communities can help to fight them and keep response teams' response realistic and helpful:

- **Optimism bias**—teams only accept what they want to hear
    For example, American weather organizations focused on the news that Hurricane Sandy was decreasing in magnitude when it passed over

the Bahamas, which would mean a less extreme storm would approach the US, preventing Americans from preparing properly when the superstorm regained strength days later.

- **Confirmation bias**—teams only accept information that reinforces existing views
    - For example, after Sandy decreased in magnitude over the Bahamas, the National Weather Service relied on a model that depicted the hurricane spinning out into the Atlantic Ocean.
- **Groupthink**—teams have a habit of agreeing with other team members
    - For example, the American weather organizations, the National Weather Service and the National Hurricane Center, agreed with one another that the hurricane would disappear over the Atlantic.
- **Solution aversion**—teams resist acknowledging a problem because they do not like the steps needed to solve it.
    - For example, the American National Weather Service took four days to approve the European model.

Leaders can combat these biases and other fears before and in the midst of a Gray Rhino crisis occurs by asking themselves the following questions:

- Am I aware of and adjusting for the biases that shape my decision to act?

    If the answer is *no*, then leaders should conduct further research on biases and/or ask trusted external individuals to provide insight. For example, the US National Weather Service also considered insight from European meteorological authorities when their models were biased toward ocean-bound storms.
- Is my team afraid to speak up about threats? Will they also stay silent about opportunities for crisis mitigation?

    If the answer is *yes*, leaders should examine and adjust their team culture to make sure their teams feel safe and confident in acknowledging and flagging potential threats. For example, a governor facing a hurricane might reiterate to local highway authorities that notification of any potential issues (e.g., bridges crumbling from the storm) both *can* and *should* be made as soon as possible. Any notifications will be heeded without repercussions to the highway authority.
- Do people around me recognize warning signs of a crisis? Do they let warnings go unheeded?

    If teams do not recognize warning signs, leaders should evaluate existing crisis preparation systems and/or invest in further training. For example, if teams are unable to detect an incoming hurricane, it may be the result of a technological issue (e.g., the weather detection system does not predict accurate storm paths) or a training issue (e.g., meteorologists do not know how to interpret the weather models). If teams recognize warning signs and let them go unheeded, see the previous question.

- Do people on my team conduct risk analyses to truly evaluate potential threats or to "check the box"?

If the answer is that teams are simply "checking a box," leaders should modify the existing threat evaluation systems to encourage preventative steps. For example, not only will weather detection agencies fine-tune their modeling systems, but they will also practice comparing models with other countries' and disseminating urgent weather information to governmental organizations.

- Do I give people credit for avoiding a preventable crisis? Or do I blame them if they do not get it right the first time?

If leaders foster a culture of blame, even for small day-to-day tasks, this will extrapolate into teams' unwillingness to come forward about larger crises. For example, a governor may credit the local transit authority with recognizing long-term fractures in highway bridges rather than berating them for not noticing sooner.

- How accurately am I weighing the costs of acting versus the costs of doing nothing?

If leaders are *inaccurately* weighing the cost of acting versus the cost of doing nothing, they will likely conclude that no action is worth taking. Even small actions can help leaders make sense of the extent of a Gray Rhino and help de-escalate its impact if it does become a crisis. For example, while rehauling an entire city's infrastructure may be more costly than doing nothing, a government may provide some funding to repair the bridges in most dire need. This will help mitigate crumbling infrastructure if a hurricane hits.

- Do I feel that I have the power to take on the problems facing me?

If the answer is *yes*, and leaders feel powerless or that the response is inadequate, they should call on other organizations to help with the response. Gray Rhino crises require complex response systems that pull from multiple organizations to resolve the issue. For example, the National Weather Service could not alone prevent or mitigate the damage that Hurricane Sandy caused. They had to call on the national government, which called on local municipalities, the Coast Guard, FEMA, and other groups to help those worst affected by the superstorm.

LEADERSHIP

When leaders face a routine crisis, they often use *linear* leadership. This leadership technique keeps leaders on "autopilot"; they move through the motions of crisis response and recreate past actions exactly. When leaders face extreme situations like Gray Rhino crises, leadership must become *nonlinear*. This means expanding upon the past as a foundation from which entirely new options can be devised and implemented to mitigate the crisis at hand.

Nonlinear leadership in a Gray Rhino crisis means helping teams as they progress through the emotional framework (outlined above in *Sensemaking*) to make sense of the situation and making decisions without the crisis response becoming affected by biases (outlined above in *Crisis Response*). Responders will not always move through this framework linearly, and leaders should be prepared to adapt to their teams' needs.

Leaders cannot respond in a "straight line"—they must be flexible enough to work independently and with other organizations toward a common goal of crisis mitigation. Some strategies for effective nonlinear leadership are outlined below.

In order to lead nonlinearly in the midst of a Black Rhino crisis, leaders should:

- Be inquisitive
- Be reflective
- Be inspired by failure
- Be resilient
- Be action-oriented

While a linear leader might assume that their experience can inform their decisions, nonlinear leaders are inquisitive. They ask questions about the situation and learn from a plurality of voices to determine the best path forward. For example, the National Weather Service did not solely rely on its own forecasting models, but instead also spoke to European meteorologists about their models to inform an effective response.

Linear leaders repeat successful crisis response patterns without stopping to consider *why* something worked. Nonlinear leaders are reflective; they think strategically about response strategies before discerning whether past tactics will serve the current response. For example, a strategic leader would consider the pros and cons of housing storm evacuees in football stadiums, like in Hurricane Katrina, and whether it would be useful in Hurricane Sandy's response before issuing orders to do so.

Linear leaders are disheartened by failure, but nonlinear leaders *use* failure to inform their response. Nonlinear leaders are experimental in their approach—if a response strategy does not work, that feedback drives their next decision. For example, New York's transit authority blocked entrances to the subway system with temporary barriers that were then blown away by Hurricane Sandy's strong winds. They used this experience to inform the development of inflatable plugs and station seals for future hurricanes.

If a leader is following a linear crisis response method and something does not go to plan, they are entirely thrown off course. Nonlinear leaders, however, are prepared for setbacks and are resilient when they happen. These leaders do not expect immediate success and they are willing to try new things when something does not work.

Linear leaders are the most likely to fall victim to a Gray Rhino because they value the safety of inaction over action. Nonlinear leaders, on the other hand, know that action is the antidote to these crises. For example, before Hurricane Sandy made landfall, leaders at FEMA deployed over 900 personnel to address power restoration, transportation, fuel distribution, and housing needs.

With their teams, leaders should be sure to:

- Listen
- Show respect
- Connect with other responders
- Develop a COP
- Establish a "battle rhythm"

Leaders should listen, show respect, and connect with their response teams. Maintaining a positive and focused attitude can help the team progress out of panic and into action more quickly. Throughout, leaders should develop a readily accessible COP that response teams can refer to at any point to know what is happening and what actions must be taken.

Establishing a "battle rhythm" means setting a response pace that keeps teams on-task and working together. This pace should be quick enough to keep the response ahead of the crisis but disciplined enough to be sustainable should the crisis continue for a long period of time. When setting the battle rhythm and responding, leaders should consider the capabilities of the organization (i.e., *What can be handled on-site? Do other response teams need to be called in for support?*). For example, the storm itself affected the American Northeast for 48 hours, but recovery efforts in New York and New Jersey lasted for nearly seven years. Emergency operations teams had to act quickly at first and then set a slow, sustainable pace to fully recover.

With outside organizations, leaders should be sure to:

- Communicate as seamlessly as possible, using the same terminology and following an ICS
- Adapt their response structure by bringing in trusted outsiders
- Develop a COP

Leaders should communicate as seamlessly as possible. This means using the same terminology and command system as other response teams taking on the crisis. Leaders facing Gray Rhinos work better when their response is shared with peers. Whether this means working with experienced teams or bringing in trusted outsiders during the response, leaders should prioritize existing relationships that will remove barriers to effective communication. With these teams, leaders should develop a COP.

With the public, leaders should be sure to:

- Communicate the reality of the crisis
- Communicate a message of resilience

Crisis response organizations may have a difficult time facing a Gray Rhino, but the public has an even more challenging time because they are so widely affected (e.g., during Hurricane Sandy, individuals in the American Northeast faced threats to their homes, communities, and lives). It is the responsibility of leaders to communicate the event to the public in a way that garners support for the response; the primary message that leaders should communicate to their teams and to the public is one of *resilience* (e.g., encouraging individuals to evacuate rather than stockpile and "hunker down"). The response teams and the public alike should have faith in the organization and community's ability to recover from the destruction the Rhino leaves in its wake.

Ultimately, failures to execute a crisis response can lead to event escalation, leading to more severe situations.

Although some information is known about the event before it occurs, leaders fail to act before a Gray Rhino crisis. To make sense of the situation, responders must begin to act and use these actions to inform the wider response. To make decisions, responders can apply past experiences *and* current data to the current situation, using macrocognition decision-making. Their organizations are not fully prepared to take on the crisis and must work with outside organizations to respond to the crisis. Leaders should be prepared to use nonlinear leadership techniques, with a focus on asking questions and learning from those around them.

While the above strategies should equip leaders to handle Gray Rhino crises, sometimes less information about an event is known and leaders are not expecting its occurrence. In this case, leaders deny the possibility that hazards will combine with vulnerabilities before they become Gray Swan crises. These will be explored in Chapter 7.

NOTE

1 Piaget, J. (1967/1971). Biology and Knowledge. Chicago University Press; and Edinburgh University Press.

Gray Swan crises

- **Situational context:** Gray Swan crises occur when the probability of an event is so low that responders deny obvious hazards even as they threaten organizational weaknesses. Information about the event is likely known and the consequences to responders and their communities are *catastrophic*.
- **Sensemaking:** Leaders can use *meta-thinking* while sensemaking to better understand a Gray Swan crisis. This means that responders begin to understand their situation by considering how they think about the information they have and the steps that they need to take to respond.
- **Decision-making:** Responders can determine how to best resolve the crisis using *functional* decision-making or assigning specific tasks to individuals/teams/organizations that work toward a common objective.
- **Crisis response:** Responders should utilize a *systems* response method which, like decision-making, assigns specific tasks to teams to work toward a common objective. Successful systems responses rely heavily on a strong integrated command system (ICS).
- **Leadership:** Leadership in a catastrophic crisis is *situational*. There is no one best way to lead, so leaders must adapt their styles to the ability and willingness of their teams to earn their trust.

DOI: 10.4324/9781003289180-7

SITUATIONAL CONTEXT

While Gray Rhinos are large, looming, and often hard to miss as they charge forward, some crises are less predictable. They can be anticipated, but the probability is so small that leaders who could prepare for the crisis deny the potential that it will ever happen. These crises are often overlooked because they are too difficult to fathom or to address. However, when leaders do not prepare for Gray Swan crises, their organizations suffer. When disaster strikes, the damage is *catastrophic*.

Key traits:

- *Information* about the event is **likely known**
- The event's *consequences* are **extreme**
- The prior *action* taken is to **deny**

The term *Gray Swan* is a byproduct of finance Professor Nassim Nicholas Taleb's *Black Swan* theory. These "cousins" of Black Swans are rare crises, but not inconceivable, so, theoretically, they can be prepared for. However, this is rarely the case. Gray Swan events require leaders to imaginatively expand upon existing data to predict and prepare for potential disasters. Gray Swans include events like financial crashes or pandemics, where warning signs manifest in statistical models early and can be mitigated if leaders are paying attention.

Despite the possibility for preparation, Gray Swans are usually unexpected and their impact is catastrophic. They can come as a surprise if warning signs are ignored, and the sooner leaders acknowledge the severity of the crisis, the quicker they can translate this understanding into action. When a Gray Swan strikes, organizations are typically unprepared and uncertain of how to act. They are unprepared because they have denied the probability of this event happening and the consequences are far more catastrophic than they have imagined. The event exceeds any past responses that the organization has performed, and therefore teams are faced with an entirely new situation.

Gray Swans are often overlooked because humans struggle to process *possibility*, often underestimating the potential of a low probability but high severity event. There are not nearly as many Gray Swans as there are Black Elephants, and they are far sneakier than Gray Rhinos. However, they are less catastrophic than Black Swans because, when they arrive, responders have more information at hand.

Case study

Deepwater Horizon as a Gray Swan crisis

On April 20, 2010, high-pressure methane gas from an oil well deep in the Gulf of Mexico rose into the Deepwater Horizon drilling rig and engulfed the platform in flames. Despite the rescue of 94 crew members and a three-day United States (US) Coast Guard search operation, 11 crew members were never found. On the morning of April 22, 2010, two days after the fire, Deepwater Horizon sank. That afternoon, a large oil slick began to spread at the former rig site. It grew into an oil spill that lasted 87 days, affecting 70,000 square miles of ocean, threatening the environment, exposing spill clean-up volunteers to poisonous compounds, and costing commercial fisheries and tourism in the area hundreds of millions of dollars.

Not only did response teams have to save lives during the fire, but they also had to track the flow of oil after the ship sank. Deepwater Horizon required the largest mobilization of resources addressing an environmental emergency in the history of the US. The US Coast Guard, the Louisiana National Guard, the National Oceanic and Atmospheric Administration (NOAA), oceanographers, scientists, British Petroleum (BP) representatives, and an army of volunteers worked together to mitigate the explosion's impacts.

The explosion, fire, collapse, and spill took the rig workers and oil industry alike by surprise; oil spills have a less than 1% chance of occurring. However, BP, the owner of Deepwater Horizon, did not take preventative measures and ignored safety warnings prior to the disaster. BP made money-saving decisions the days before the accident and continued to drill in spite of warnings of a gas leak, dramatically increasing the potential for a crisis. The consequences of the spill were extreme and the potential for this event was denied. Because the probability of this disaster was small, but some information was known, this event is not a Gray Rhino or Black Swan, but a Gray Swan.

SENSEMAKING

Leaders facing a Gray Swan will face sensemaking challenges as teams grapple with reality and decide how to respond. There is typically some information available about a Gray Swan, providing leaders with a starting point from which to respond. Leaders should use both this data and *meta-thinking* strategies to begin to make sense of the situation.

Meta-thinking means thinking about how to think. Leaders should consider what information they need to make sense of the situation and should use their imagination to predict what decisions they will have to make as the crisis response progresses. In this way, leaders can make sense of actionable items and begin to craft a response.

As responders make sense of their surroundings, leaders should be aware of cognitive biases that can impact understanding the situation. Recognizing these potential biases and applying meta-thinking to form a solution can help to fight them and keep response teams' sensemaking realistic and helpful.

- **Normalcy bias**—teams underestimate the likelihood and severity of disaster scenarios. Likely, this perception might lead to a lack of mitigation before a Gray Swan situation, but it can also impact responders' understanding of the situation by limiting their ability to process what has happened.

  For example, two hours before the explosion, BP's Vice President of drilling was onboard Deepwater Horizon, celebrating seven years without a safety incident. So, when equipment readings began to indicate gas bubbling into the well, onboard crew members felt safe and followed the planned protocol that made it easier for gas to bubble up and explode.

  Leaders can mitigate normalcy bias by heeding warning signs and, once a disaster has occurred, publicly acknowledging the reality of the crisis and its potential for escalation. Leaders become aware of potential disasters and escalation by meta-thinking: *What could happen? What do I know about the situation? What do I not know?* If leaders actively ask and answer these questions before and during a Gray Swan crisis, they will be able to better prepare their organizations and teams for a response.

- **Ambiguity effect**—teams prefer options with known probabilities and may avoid options with less information because they seem riskier. Likely, this aversion will affect decision-making, but it can also impact responders' understanding of the situation by limiting what information they seek about the disaster as they decide how to proceed.

  For example, BP almost primarily used surface oil dispersants to break down the oil. Oil dispersants were the preferred option because information about them was already known and dispersants had been used before to mitigate oil spill impacts. Unknown options were not explored in-depth, despite the pitfalls of dispersants (including extreme damage to marine life).

Leaders can mitigate the ambiguity effect by actively learning more about the situation and potential solutions *before* making decisions. Leaders should use meta-thinking to be conscious of not only what decision they are making but *why* they are making it: *What do I know about this situation? What do I know about this potential solution? Why am I leaning toward choosing this option over another one?* If leaders actively ask and answer these questions while trying to understand the situation, they will be prepared to respond most appropriately to the crisis' demands.

• **Optimism bias**—teams *under*estimate the likelihood of being directly affected by the crisis and *over*estimate the potential for a positive experience; this leads to the systematic miscalculation of the probabilities of accidents. When affected by optimism, responders at all levels will make decisions that do not match the reality of the crisis. Before a Gray Swan crisis, optimism bias will have a similar effect as normalcy bias. However, *after* a crisis has occurred, optimism bias typically affects leaders who are the furthest away from the crisis site, as they have a limited understanding of what is happening on the ground.

For example, the explosion was initially a result of optimism in the safety of Deepwater Horizon's well. If BP had less trust in their systems in advance of the crisis, it likely would not have occurred. After the explosion and spill, BP executives continued to have misplaced faith in their on-the-ground mitigation efforts, believing—despite many failed attempts to stop the spill—that the oil leak had been plugged using a tightly fitted cap. However, four days after BP announced the leak had been stopped, seepage was detected on site yet again.

Leaders can mitigate optimism bias by making past negative events more easily retrievable from one's memory and by highlighting losses that are likely to occur because of past events. Leaders can use meta-thinking to do this: *What negative events have happened before? What decisions have I made that have made bad situations worse/better? How do past events impact the current situation? What losses are likely to occur in this crisis?* If leaders actively ask and answer these questions, they will be able to tether their optimism to some negative experiences. Leaders can also get physically nearer to the crisis site and/or talk to on-scene actors to bring their understanding of the situation closer to reality.

Felt emotions

Felt emotions play a powerful role in Gray Swan crises. As situations become more extreme, as they typically do in a catastrophic crisis, a responder's awareness of impending death, also called *mortality salience*, impacts that person's ability to think. As mortality salience increases, cognition decreases. Even if a responder has high cognitive abilities, they are not likely to suppress mortality salience (more information on *mortality salience* can be found in Chapter 4). Some cognitive biases to be aware of as felt emotions and mortality salience arise in a Gray Swan crisis are:

- **Ostrich effect**—teams ignore negative information to avoid the anxiety of decision-making or understanding reality; this will only escalate a crisis situation.

  For example, BP engineers onboard Deepwater Horizon ignored an abnormal pressure reading because the potential consequences were anxiety inducing. Instead, they proceeded with an operation to remove mud (which was holding down the gas) and replace it with seawater (which made it easier for gas to bubble and explode).

  Leaders can mitigate the ostrich effect by taking small, actionable steps and asking questions to better understand the negative information. Actionable steps might be physical tasks (e.g., shutting down oil pumps) or verbal tasks (e.g., notifying a higher-ranking engineer of abnormal readings). Asking questions to better understand the situation involves meta-thinking: *Although I am uncomfortable, what information must I know to make an informed decision in this situation?* If leaders embrace the anxiety of uncertainty in Gray Swan crises, they can begin to fill in the gaps in their understanding and better prepare to respond.

- **Herd instinct**—teams align with the behavior of the larger group to avoid conflict.

  For example, crew members aboard Deepwater Horizon were afraid of mentioning potential dangers or abnormalities. Because of this desire to avoid potential conflict, when risky materials were used and system readings reached dangerous levels, the problems were not adequately reported.

  Leaders can take on herd instinct by ensuring that individual points of view are valued in the workplace. They should use meta-thinking to consider how their teams think and act: *What are the unspoken rules among the team that should be acknowledged? What biases do we have?* When leaders recognize unspoken assumptions, they should discuss them openly. Leaders should also be sure not to punish individuals that bring forward new ideas or disagree with the group. Treating all team members with respect and valuing people's opinions are key attributes of creating a transparent work environment that resolves conflicts more quickly.

• **Status quo bias**—teams prefer to continue using normal protocol rather than risk loss.

⚠️ For example, the day of the Deepwater Horizon explosion, crew members continued with usual procedures despite warning signs like concerning pipeline pressure readings, fluid flow rates, and cement work around the pipe. Their adherence to status quo procedures led to less preparation before the explosion that could have mitigated its catastrophic consequences.

Leaders can counter status quo bias by framing the alternative option to maintaining the status quo as a loss. This means that instead of saying, "If we change our actions, we risk loss" leaders say, "If we *do not* change our actions, we will lose." Leaders can utilize metathinking by considering what their teams might fear: *What losses are at stake? What are we risking by not acting?* If leaders use the answers to these questions to frame the situation, they will be better prepared to take on a Gray Swan crisis.

DECISION-MAKING

Gray Swans often require multiple organizations to form one emergency operations center that makes key decisions. In the face of extreme situations, leaders must make decisions that ascribe *functions* to all participating response organizations that mitigate the crisis as quickly as possible. This means setting a singular objective (e.g., reducing the impact of an oil spill) and assigning individuals, teams, or organizations specific tasks/duties that will work toward that goal (e.g., one organization may focus on plugging the leak while other teams remove oil from the ocean).

Theoretical background: Functional decision-making

In functional decision-making processes, actions are predetermined and assigned to certain actors. These tasks are specific and goal-oriented and distributed through a linear hierarchy of responders. The flow of decision-making in a Gray Swan crisis is initially top down—leaders at the emergency operations center provide orders to lower levels of command. The lower levels then send detailed feedback about the crisis situation back up the chain of command which is used to inform the next high-level decisions.

Practical advice: How to make decisions in a Gray Swan crisis

When situations are uncertain and do not have much information, leaders at the decision-making level should refer to similar events or past experiences. These can provide a basis from which to make decisions when there is no other information. For example, the first information that responders received from Deepwater Horizon was a report of fire on board. Leaders, despite having sparse information about this specific crisis, were able to initiate protocols developed from prior experiences with rig fires and begin the process of rescuing the crew on the rig. Once decision makers heard from on-scene actors that the cause of the flames was an oil leak, the response was adjusted accordingly (i.e., leaders assigned response organizations the task of stopping the leak).

There are some important considerations as leaders make decisions in the emergency operations center. Leaders should NOT:

- Delay action
- Submit to panic
- Overlook important issues while *in media res*
- Chase after unimportant information or data
- Second guess, change strategy unnecessarily, or lack confidence
- Overcommit to one solution instead of evaluating multiple options

---

Gray Swans are catastrophic, typically fast-paced events. Leaders should be sure to make quick decisions and do their best not to delay action by trying to gather too much information. Once decisions are made, on-scene actors will begin to provide feedback that informs further decisions. Decision makers should do their best not to submit to panic. Panicked decisions are not strategic or functional; they are typically made on-site and do not incorporate other actors. If leaders are properly utilizing functional decision-making, decisions will incorporate other actors and will be made from the emergency response center.

On the ground, responders can get distracted by responding to one element of the crisis and miss larger, more important issues. While having an emergency operations center does have drawbacks of increased optimism bias, it can be beneficial in maintaining a distance and seeing the "bigger picture." Leaders can also use this perspective to prevent chasing after unimportant information and data.

Decision makers should be confident in their decisions. Second-guessing and strategy changes will only confuse responders as decisions travel down to on-scene actors. However, leaders should also be mindful not to overcommit to one solution. Leaders can balance confidence and overcommitment through trial and error: Once a decision has been decided, executed, and feedback from on-scene actors has been received, decision makers can use that information to modify, adjust, and shape future strategies.

CRISIS RESPONSE

Gray Swan crises require a *systems* response. This crisis response method aligns with functional decision-making discussed above; it means multiple, separate organizations perform specific actions to mitigate the crisis. These functions might be outside of the organization's typical purview, but response teams must adapt to the demands of the disaster rather than operating using a routine response strategy. For example, while BP typically acted as the primary managers of the Deepwater Horizon rig, when the oil spill began, they had to expand their responsibilities and work with the Coast Guard to stop the leaking.

A systems response requires a well-built ICS. If response organizations do not have a predetermined ICS, creating a clear hierarchical command structure should be a top priority (for more information on ICSs, see Chapter 4). At the emergency operations center, leaders should develop a primary objective and a list of what must be done to achieve it. Tasks on the list should be assigned to response teams throughout the ICS as necessary.

To design a systems response, leaders should:

- Set an objective
- Make a list of operational priorities and supplies needed
- Assess the capabilities of all on-site responders
- Assess the capabilities of other involved organizations and leaders
- Anchor decisions in facts when possible

Leaders should start their crisis response by setting an objective; the crisis response should contribute toward this goal. This goal can change as the situation evolves. For example, the responders at Deepwater Horizon initially set a goal of saving the people on board but later prioritized stopping the oil leak and, even later, focused on cleaning the ocean.

To begin the crisis response, leaders should make a list of operational priorities and supplies needed. For example, if the overarching goal is to save crew members from a fire on board, the operational priorities might be to move people safely from the flames to hospitals. This would require additional supplies like helicopters, ropes, and ambulances.

Leaders would then assess the capabilities of on-site responders. Continuing the Deepwater Horizon example, the on-site responders were struggling for air, unable to escape the flames. They did not have access to a helicopter or any other quick method to get injured crewmen to land.

When on-site responders are unable to help themselves, crisis response leaders must assess the capabilities of other organizations and leaders that might be able to help. In Deepwater Horizon's case, the Coast Guard was nearby and had access to helicopters that could safely transport the crew away from the rig.

A Gray Swan likely has some information available, so crisis response should be based on these facts when possible. For example, the response decision to call in the Coast Guard was based on the knowledge that members aboard Deepwater Horizon needed to exit quickly and they did not have the means to do so, while the Coast Guard did.

LEADERSHIP

There is no best way to lead a team through a catastrophic event, especially a crisis that involves impending death. Therefore, straightforward and routine linear leadership methods should be set aside so that leaders can adapt, using on-the-ground, *situational* leadership strategies.

Situational leadership theory argues that effective leadership is task-relevant, and the most successful leaders adapt their styles to the ability and willingness of their teams. Leadership varies both by the task at hand but also by the teams who are asked to complete the task. This theory combines leadership style (i.e., *how* a leader is leading) and their teams' readiness level (i.e., how *able and willing* a group is to act).

According to situational leadership theory, there are four leadership styles: *Delegating, participating, selling,* and *telling.* None of these styles are considered useful in all scenarios, and they should be used interchangeably as leaders adapt to the scenario at hand.

- **Delegating**—leaders give most of the responsibility to their team. They monitor progress but let teams make decisions and act on their own.

  For example, leaders on Deepwater Horizon assigned the responsibility of lowering the lifeboats to certain team members so that individuals on board could safely escape the flames.

  "Lower the boats!"
  – National Commission on the BP Deepwater Oil Spill

- **Participating**—leaders focus more on relationships than on providing instructions. They work with the team to share decision-making responsibilities.

  For example, leaders on Deepwater Horizon boarded emergency lifeboats alongside their teams, helping individuals into the boats and helping guide them to safety.

  "We are not going to leave you here." – National Commission on the BP Deepwater Oil Spill

- **Selling**—leaders provide direction and spend time persuading their teams to agree with their decision.

  For example, when some individuals did not want to board lifeboats, leaders coaxed them to safety.

  "Hey, where are you going? There's a perfectly good boat here. Do you trust me?"
  – National Commission on the BP Deepwater Oil Spill

- **Telling**—leaders tell their teams what to do and how to do it.

  For example, leaders on Deepwater Horizon commanded their teams to board emergency lifeboats.

  "Report to emergency lifeboats. This is not a drill."
  – National Commission on the BP Deepwater Oil Spill

None of the above leadership styles is one-size-fits-all and finding the right leadership style will also depend on the team's readiness to act. In situational leadership theory, team readiness can be measured on a four-point scale:

- **Low maturity**—teams lack the skills, knowledge, or confidence to work on their own. These teams are often unwilling to take on tasks.
- **Medium maturity, low skills**—teams are willing to do the task but do not have the skills to complete it successfully.

- **Medium maturity, higher skills**—teams are ready and willing to do the task. They have the skills to complete it successfully, but they lack confidence in their abilities.
- **High maturity**—teams are able to do the task on their own and are confident in their ability to do it well. They are willing and able to do the task and to take responsibility for the outcome.

Maturity levels are task-specific; a team may be generally skilled, confident, and willing to work but still might have low maturity when asked to perform a task they are unfamiliar with or if it is in a catastrophic crisis situation. Effective leaders are able to navigate the various leadership styles and maturity levels and capitalize on crisis resolution when their teams are at high maturity.

One way for leaders to capitalize on crisis resolution is to build trust with their teams. In Gray Swan crises, there is often a point when workers are fearful of their lives and reassess their level of trust in the leader. After that threshold comes a constant reassessment of trust in the leaders. In these dangerous contexts, trust is a function of how well a leader performs. Trust is built when leaders have high, but realistic expectations of their teams. Supportive relationships between the leader and their teams, or loyalty, is key to a smooth response. Trust and loyalty go hand-in-hand when responding to a Gray Swan.

To build trust, leaders must:

- Embrace continuous learning from their teams
- Develop a common operational perspective (COP)
- Share risks with their teams
- Maintain a common lifestyle
- Emphasize shared values
- Possess technical competence
- Exhibit loyalty

Leaders should continue to gather information from their teams throughout a Gray Swan response. They should use information from on-scene responders and other response organizations to form a common operational perspective of the situation (see Chapter 4 for more information on COPs). Having a shared understanding of the crisis situation allows leaders and their teams to communicate more clearly. For example, leaders at Deepwater Horizon frequently talked to people who were on board and generated a COP at their emergency operations center.

Leaders should share risks with and maintain a common lifestyle with their teams. For example, if teams are out clearing oil from the ocean and exposing themselves to potentially harmful chemicals, leaders should be too. If teams are eating in a mess hall while out at the rig, leaders should be too. To earn trust, leaders should ensure that they do not think—or act like—they are "better" than their teams.

Leaders should emphasize shared values and possess technical competence. Leaders should highlight when they have similar priorities to their teams (e.g., "I also miss my family"). Leaders should also be technically competent—on-scene responders will be quick to notice if those in leadership positions do not know what they are talking about. For example, people directing engineers at Deepwater Horizon also knew oil rig terminology and operations.

If a leader wants trust, they must display trust. The key to building loyalty is to *be* loyal. Leaders do this by having a "no one left behind" mentality and making sacrifices for their teams when necessary. For example, leaders aboard Deepwater Horizon waited for their teams to safely board lifeboats before boarding themselves.

Although some information is likely known about the event before it occurs, leaders deny that a Gray Swan will occur and the results are catastrophic. To make sense of the situation, responders must think about decisions that they might have to make in order to inform the wider response. To make decisions, responders can assign specific tasks to designated teams, working slowly to decide how to resolve the crisis. Organizations are not fully prepared to take on the crisis and must work with outside organizations, typically using an ICS, to respond to the crisis. Leaders should be prepared to adapt their leadership styles to the ability and willingness of the team to complete tasks.

While the above strategies should equip leaders to handle Gray Swan crises, sometimes the completely unfathomable occurs. In this case, leaders have no idea that hazards and vulnerabilities could possibly combine to create a Black Swan crisis. These will be explored in Chapter 8.

Black Swan crises

- **Situational context:** Black Swan crises are entirely unfathoma-ble. These crises catch organizations by surprise—no information about the event is known in advance, so no preparatory action has been taken before these *extreme* events occur.
- **Sensemaking:** Leaders can use a *common operational per-spective* while sensemaking to better understand a Black Swan crisis. This means that responders create a single display of relevant information to be shared by more than one emergency operations center to facilitate collaborative planning and understanding.
- **Decision-making:** Responders must determine how to best resolve the crisis *in situ*, using *unified* decision-making that considers the confidence and abilities of all teams and organizations involved to make choices.
- **Crisis response:** Responders should utilize an *integrated* response method which incorporates many multi-level organi-zations to respond to the crisis. Successful integrated responses rely heavily on a strong integrated command system (ICS).
- **Leadership:** Leaders in an extreme crisis must be *warriors*. There is no one best way to lead, so leaders must focus on forming trusting, strong relationships with their teams.

SITUATIONAL CONTEXT

Imagine a town beside a river. For as long as anyone has known, only white swans have floated down the stream. But one day, a black swan passes through. The townspeople have no frame of reference for this—its existence alone is

DOI: 10.4324/9781003289180-8

incomprehensible. Similar to the town, organizations regularly face White Swan crises. However, very rarely, leaders can be caught entirely by surprise with the arrival of an unfathomable event: The Black Swan crisis. The challenge in these types of crises is inherent—similar to the town beside the river, organizations have had no way of predicting that a Black Swan crisis might occur, so there is no information about the event and no way to prepare for its arrival. The result is an *extreme* situation.

Key traits:

- *Information* about the event is **unknown**
- The event's *consequences* are **unfathomable**
- There is **little, insufficient,** or **no preparedness**

The rarity of the Black Swan crises in relation to the frequency of White Swan crises is why finance professor and former Wall Street trader, Nassim Nichols Taleb, coined the term. Black Swan crises are events that are entirely impossible to predict and are so rare that even the probability of their occurrence is unknown to leaders. They cause chaos regardless of preparation strategy or training and experience; Black Swan crises are not caused by leadership failures, but by unfathomable and uncontrollable external forces. Regardless, it is worthwhile to consider leadership strategy prior to a Black Swan crisis so, if disaster strikes, leaders are prepared to respond and return to the familiar as quickly as possible.

Black Swans are unique in their unpredictability and danger. Leaders face events with varying degrees of predictability, discussed earlier in the *Black Elephant, Gray Rhino,* and *Gray Swan* chapters. There are not nearly as many Black Swan crises as there are Black Elephant, Gray Rhino, or even Gray Swan crises combined. Black Swans are often called "one-percent events," because they comprise less than 1% of all crises. If an event's consequences are extreme and no preparatory action has been taken, but it can be predicted, it is not a Black Swan (see Chapter 7 on Gray Swans instead).

Case study

The Fukushima nuclear disaster as a Black Swan crisis

☢ On March 11, 2011, an earthquake struck the Tohoku Region in eastern Japan. A 9.0 earthquake, its effects were felt as far away as Antarctica.

The tsunami it created was enormous. Ocean waves as high as four and five story buildings overwhelmed villages up and down the Sendai Coast. Roads, bridges, homes, and buildings fell, swept away by the waves in just minutes. Tens of thousands of lives were lost.

Soon, Japanese nuclear plants Fukushima-Daiichi and Daini were without vital water and power supplies. Without this lifeblood, the reactors and spent fuel pools threatened meltdown. Nuclear meltdowns can release radioactive materials into the environment, poisoning all life in the vicinity. However, most of the emergency equipment, facilities, and people in the area that could help mitigate this crisis were lost to the earthquake and tsunami. The situation had surpassed the fathomable. The international community mobilized to help Japan rescue the living, recover the lost, repair the heavily damaged infrastructure, and prevent nuclear meltdown.

The Fukushima Disaster surpassed a Gray Swan crisis because the combination of the earthquakes and tsunami's effects on the nuclear plant was entirely unpredictable, and the leadership and response teams were completely unprepared to take on the crisis. The consequences were extremely dangerous for both leaders and the surrounding population, threatening their lives and communities as they tried to return to the status quo.

SENSEMAKING

At its core, sensemaking is about taking cues from the environment and framing those cues to form a perspective of what is transpiring. However, humans naturally seek to simplify complex events, which can lead to responders missing important signals that can inform the crisis response. Especially in a Black Swan event, leaders and their teams alike will struggle to grasp reality, making other crisis response sensemaking theories (i.e., *updating, enacted, metathinking*) ineffective. As response teams face death (or experience *mortality salience,* as discussed in Chapter 4), their perception of the situation will be restricted as cognitive abilities narrow. To counter the urge to simplify the situation, leaders should instead seek to understand the Black Swan crisis' full complexities. This can be done by using a *common operational perspective* (COP) as a sensemaking process. While it is more difficult than in other crises, the development of a COP is crucial in a Black Swan crisis. With a COP, leaders can build on their sensemaking by consistently working toward broader understanding of the events.

Though COPs can often be a *product*, such as a map of the crisis site, they can also be a *process*. In this process, responders can forge a common reality in an information-starved and ever-changing environment by continuously compiling information into a widely shared and accessible COP. Responders share and give meaning to information, using standardized terminology and consistently updated information to synchronize their actions. For example, during the Fukushima crisis, international responders created a COP through the impromptu use of the *Hosono Process*. This series of regular intergovernmental meetings was named after the lead Japanese official orchestrating the response, Goshi Hosono, who moderated these daily coordination sessions that included all relevant agencies from both Japan and the US. At these meetings, project teams were set up on topics like shielding nuclear materials and disposal of contaminated materials; this facilitated discussions on the needs of each area of the response and unified situational knowledge of the crisis by coordinating requests for information and material from the Japanese to the international community.

To sensemake and develop a COP in the midst of a Black Swan crisis, leaders should set their primary goals as: *Gathering meaningful information, combining other sensemaking strategies,* and *improving situational understanding.*

To gather meaningful information, leaders should:

- Ask purposeful questions
- Understand where information is coming from, how to process and make sense of it
- Find ways to inject coherent information despite unreliable data

---

Leaders should ask questions with *purpose* that will shed light on the situation. These questions should be intentional and rooted in informing the response. Leaders should prioritize the kinds of questions based on their relevance to understanding the situation. For example, asking which nuclear reactors need water is important because it informs where fire trucks should be sent. On the other hand, asking unnecessary questions like "What model of firetruck are you sending?" distracts from the response.

Information in a Black Swan crisis is sparse. When information is gathered, leaders should know the sources (and how reliable they are). They should also know how to process, understand, and use the information. For example, knowing which nuclear reactor needs water is useful if leaders know who to inform to resolve the issue.

Leaders play a key role in information processing in a Black Swan crisis by making sense of unreliable information. Expertise and experience become increasingly relevant as information is less coherent. While gathering information from their teams, leaders should actively incorporate logical understanding to organize thoughts into a COP. Leaders should be sure that extraneous information is not provided without context; to do this, leaders can ask themselves *"Why should my teams know this?"* before sharing information. Leaders should develop a list of priorities for each level of the response; for example, assigning local emergency response teams the responsibility of day-to-day medical support and federal emergency response teams the responsibility of mitigating nuclear radiation.

To combine other sensemaking strategies, leaders should:
- *Act* their way toward sense
- Use *meta-thinking* to think about thinking

While enacted sensemaking *alone* is not adequate to generate understanding in a Black Swan crisis, it can be used alongside other sensemaking strategies. *Enacted* sensemaking means that crisis responders begin to understand the context of their situation by acting. These do not need to be big, complex actions, but rather small, simple tasks that work toward mitigating the crisis. Enacted sensemaking follows the logic that taking even small steps can clarify what the solution may be. For example, on the evening of March 11, 2011, government officials ordered an evacuation of residents within 2km of the Fukushima Nuclear Plant. By the following evening, leaders issued evacuation orders for residents within a 20km radius. Though the initial evacuation order was not nearly large or comprehensive enough to be the solution, it started a crisis response that could clarify the severity of the situation and be built upon with more expansive evacuation orders.

Meta-thinking is another sensemaking strategy that can be used in conjunction with enacted sensemaking to build a COP in a Black Swan event. Meta-thinking means thinking about how to think. Leaders should consider what information they need to make sense of the situation and should use their imagination to predict what decisions they will have to make as the crisis response progresses. In this way, leaders can create actionable tasks and begin to craft a response. For example, leaders at Fukushima were aware that they might have to shut down schools even months after the initial accident and thinking about the need to make these decisions helped to put preparatory plans in place. Radiation can have more extreme effects for children, so responders knew that they would have to evaluate potential contamination in schools. Because of the size and the severity of the issue, leaders worked with the Ministry of Education to create radiation guidelines and radiation measurement systems as well as public service announcements and manuals to guide individuals on decontamination practices.

To improve situational understanding, leaders should:

- Discourage their teams (and themselves) from isolated perspectives
- Hold onto a healthy skepticism
- Update the COP as events develop

No single responder can *respond* to a Black Swan crisis by themselves; in the same way, no single responder can make *sense* of a Black Swan crisis on their own. Leaders should discourage their teams (and themselves) from isolated perspectives, or the notion that one individual should have a unique understanding of the crisis. To do this, leaders should emphasize the development of a COP and source information and perspectives from all members of their team. For example, during the Fukushima crisis response, American engineers received information directly from Japanese engineers who received their information from Japanese middle-level managers; this left the American engineers with less and later information than their Japanese counterparts. This isolation led to confusion and mistrust that obscured a more developed picture of the situation until American leaders forged a relationship with the Japanese middle-level managers.

Leaders should also maintain a healthy skepticism. This means overcoming optimism bias (the underestimation of negative consequences). Optimism has a place in extreme crisis management as a motivation to act; however, it can create blind spots and prevent individuals from adapting to new circumstances. Leaders can mitigate optimism bias by retrieving memories of past events, even if the outcomes were negative, and highlighting losses that are likely to occur if events progress in a similar way. Leaders can use meta-thinking to do this: *What negative events have happened before? What decisions have I made that have made bad situations worse/better? How do past events impact the current situation? What losses are likely to occur in this crisis?* If leaders actively ask and answer these questions, they will be able to constrain their optimism with realistic, negative experiences. For example, nuclear plants use computer simulators to train their operators for a nuclear crisis. This training builds confidence, but it also builds blind spots. Prior to the Fukushima nuclear crisis, the operators were trained on a simulator for extreme crisis events, including the nuclear meltdown that befell them. However, the training stopped just short of a major catastrophe. So, when the unfathomable occurred, operators were overoptimistic and underprepared for a response.

In Black Swan crises, COPs are an evolving process. Leaders should be sure to continuously update the COP as the event progresses. When new information is learned, it should be compiled by the emergency operations center where it can be accessed widely among all participating organizations. Not all information needs to be actively shared; leaders should use their discretion to determine what to actively share with teams. This differs from other crisis types, where information sharing can be used as a tool for trust building. For example, when the Fukushima nuclear accident first occurred, the government hypothesized a worst-case scenario in which evacuations would need to be conducted within 250km of the site. While it was important for officials to plan for such an event, sharing this information with the public engendered unnecessary distrust and anxiety among the Japanese public.

FELT EMOTIONS

The mindset of a leader in a Black Swan crisis is the most primed for failure because the event has challenged all understanding of what is possible, leaving responders aghast and afraid. However, if leaders are aware that their felt emotions pose a threat to their ability to make sense of the situation and respond, they are better able to acknowledge and overcome emotional barriers, especially within their teams.

During a Black Swan crisis, mortality salience overpowers most other felt emotions—responders are acutely aware that their lives are in danger. This results in a cognitive narrowing or a limiting of responders' ability to think. Set procedures, authority, and morality are set aside in favor of an intuitive mindset that prioritizes self-preservation over the "greater good." Self-preservation can lead to defiance that hinders the crisis response. For example, at Fukushima, firefighters sent to help control the reactor's water levels to save the wider community from nuclear fallout stopped working due to a fear of high radiation levels near the fire trucks.

However, intuitive thinking and self-preservation can be strategically managed to benefit the crisis response. Leaders can offset fear with more positive emotions, like drawing on responders' sense of duty and identifying the shared struggle. For example, at Fukushima, operators wanted to abandon the on-site control room. Leaders bowed and apologized to the operators, asking them to stay and promising that leadership would defy higher-ranking commands that put the operators' lives at risk if conditions became too dangerous. This appeal worked and operators remained in the control room to control the fire.

The operators' desire to leave the control room is an example of *constructive defiance*, or intuitive actions taken by responders under dangerous conditions that are contrary to the desires of their leader but are in the best interest of the responders directly faced by extreme conditions. Constructive defiance implies that responders who face dangerous conditions might ignore all directions or encouragement offered by the leader and succumb to their own self-interest. The leaders in the control room situation navigated this by framing what they needed their teams to do (stay in the control room to fight the fire) by capitalizing on self-preservation (appealing to the operators' sense of duty and promising safety).

Strong, and largely negative, felt emotions in a Black Swan crisis are unavoidable and should not be ignored. It is up to leaders to understand both their own emotions and those of their team and engage in techniques to make sense of the situation and thwart undesirable, emotion-driven actions.

DECISION-MAKING

Decision making in a Black Swan crisis is unique compared to other crises because it is almost entirely done *in situ*. It breaks from traditional models of leadership and decision-making by often requiring the on-site responder to make moral judgments, including defying orders that do not actively resolve the crisis or that challenge responders' intuitive self-interest, as explained above. Leaders must maintain focus and stay ahead of the situation because allowing a Black Swan to escalate can quickly overwhelm any response systems available. The priority in a Black Swan should be to make *unified* decisions that use all parts of the coordinated response to mitigate the crisis.

Theoretical background: Unified decision-making

The lack of time and information in a Black Swan crisis renders decision-making based upon optimal solutions unlikely. Therefore, research suggests that leaders should focus on making precise *decisions* rather than working toward precise solutions. To do this, leaders should be mindful of the factors that decisions are based on *difficulty* and *confidence*.

The difficulty of the decision and the confidence of the responder or leader in that decision together influence decision-making precision. Leaders are typically more confident in less difficult decisions. For example, responders facing a building on fire are confident in deciding to extinguish the fire as opposed to responders facing a nuclear blazing reactor who are less confident in exposing themselves to radiation while extinguishing a more complex fire.

The strain of the situation affects decision-making difficulty because the more extreme the crisis, the more difficult the decision will be in terms of technical difficulty, potential danger, felt emotions, and other factors that may increase complexity in decision-making.

Confidence can be summarized as *self-efficacy*. Self-efficacy can be defined as a responder's *judgment* of their capability to organize and execute courses of action that lead to a result. It is not an actual assessment of skills, but rather a measure of a responder's or leader's perception of their abilities. Self-efficacy can be conditioned by prior successes or similar experiences that contribute to their decision-making capabilities.

Practical advice: How to make decisions in a Black Swan crisis

In a Black Swan, leaders should:

- Make decisions based on the best information available
- Seek out broader points of view
- Learn from history
- Act their way into decision-making
- Look for obvious solutions
- Focus on timing
- Assess where established procedures can be circumvented
- Prioritize all responders in terms of their ability to achieve the goal
- Focus on *system* failures rather than *effort* failures
- Strive to understand what others are thinking
- Debate outside of formal meetings
- Only share necessary information

Black Swan crises are information-starved environments. Leaders are caught entirely unprepared by the unfathomable event. As leaders gather information about the event, they should seek broader points of view from responders at all levels (on and off-site) to inform the COP. The COP can then be used to inform decisions. For example, leaders at Fukushima received on-site information from engineers about which nuclear reactors had lost power and off-site information from weather services about the tsunami's impacts. This information was combined together as leaders created a COP to inform the response.

When deciding, leaders should consider the response organizations involved and determine *who* can contribute *what* to the crisis response. Involved organizations should be prioritized in the decision-making process based on their ability to accomplish the goal. For example, during the Fukushima crisis, responders needed to inject water to the pools that cooled the nuclear fuel. There was a debate over whether the fire department, the police, or the military should add the water. The fire department argued that they could spray water upward during the response to the fire, while the police argued that they could use crowd control methods to spray water. The military argued that they could drop water from the sky using a helicopter. After the debate, the decision was made to first use the military and if that did not work, then to use the fire department, then the police department.

Leaders should learn from history—not only should leaders gather data as the event progresses, but they should also look to past events to inform their current decisions. In line with enacted sensemaking (discussed above), leaders should *act* their way into decision-making. This means deciding, acting on it, and then using information from the result to evaluate and recalibrate the response. This iterative process will inform future decisions. One way to act into decision-making is to look for obvious solutions and act on these first. Obvious solutions provide a strong starting point for feedback and information gathering. Additionally, timing is key. Any decisions that are made should prioritize timing. For example, if a solution is attempted (e.g., dousing the nuclear reactors with water from the sky only), the responders should develop success criteria (e.g., is the water from the sky enough to cool the reactor? Is the reactor cooling?) and a timeline for the solution (e.g., if the reactor is not cooled within the hour, it will be necessary for firefighters to douse the reactors from the ground).

Leaders should also be prepared to circumvent established procedures to expand the organization's ability to respond to the crisis. For example, if shutting off a reactor requires multiple levels of approval, leaders should be prepared to approve it early and without following established protocol.

Decisions that leaders make should focus on *system* failures rather than *effort* failures; leaders should assume that all responders are doing their best under the circumstances. This means that rather than pushing their teams to respond "better," leaders will make strategic decisions that improve the response. To make high-level system decisions, leaders should strive to understand what their teams are thinking and what constraints they perceive. These constraints can provide the basis for strategy changes.

Leaders should debate decisions outside of and before formal meetings rather than during meetings. Leaders should also be careful about what information is shared with whom. While response organizations need an information-dense COP, it should only incorporate necessary information. Debating decisions during meetings and infusing decisions with extraneous information can cause confusion for responders and expose organizational weaknesses that break down trust. For example, during the Fukushima crisis, misinformation was rampant; online videos created by "experts" made its way into conversations leaders were having while developing the COP. This became a huge distraction that resulted in the unnecessary evacuation of a number of US citizens from Japan.

Leaders should not:

- Delay action
- Chase after information or data that are not important
- Submit to panic
- Overlook important issues while *in media res*
- Second-guess, make unnecessary strategy changes, or lack confidence
- Overcommit to one solution
- Rely on "imperial intervention," or well-meaning higher-ups providing unhelpful direction
- Defer to expertise alone, without considering other factors

---

Black Swans are extreme, fast-paced events. Leaders should be sure to make quick decisions and do their best not to delay action by trying to gather *too* much information. Once decisions are made, on-scene actors will begin to provide feedback that informs further decisions.

Decision makers should do their best not to submit to panic. Panicked decisions are not strategic or functional; they are typically made on-site and do not incorporate other actors. If leaders are properly utilizing functional decision-making, decisions will incorporate other actors and will be made from the emergency response center.

On the ground, responders can get distracted by responding to one crisis and miss larger, more important issues. Leaders should maintain a mental distance from the event and try to see the "bigger picture." Leaders can also use this perspective to prevent chasing after unimportant information and data.

Decision makers should be confident in their decisions. Second-guessing and strategy changes will only confuse responders as decisions travel down through to on-scene actors. However, leaders should also be mindful to not to overcommit to one solution. Leaders can balance confidence and overcommitment through trial and error: Once a decision has been decided, executed, and feedback from on-scene actors has been received, decision makers can use that information to modify, adjust, and shape future strategies.

Black Swan crises require a multi-level response, typically involving national or even international crisis management organizations. Though this substantial mobilization of resources can be helpful, leaders are more exposed to "imperial intervention." Imperial intervention happens when well-intentioned leaders (typically located far away from the crisis site) provide unhelpful direction. In these scenarios, on-site leaders should use their best judgment to direct their teams with the understanding that they will have to justify their transgressions to higher-ups later.

CRISIS RESPONSE

When a Black Swan strikes, organizations are uncertain and unprepared. Leaders are uncertain because information about the event is unavailable and/or evolving. Leaders are unprepared because no prior training has adequately prepared responders to take on this crisis, and the crisis cannot be handled by one organization on its own. Response organizations must work together in an *integrated* response, combining their capabilities to meet the demands of the Black Swan crisis. While leaders might not know much about a Black Swan situation, they know they must respond. In these low-information circumstances, more chaos will inevitably arise. The goal of a crisis response is to reduce chaos and return to the familiar, so responders must work together to gather information and act.

While COPs help crisis response organizations *make sense* of the surroundings, ICSs help organizations *respond* to them. COPs help to prevent missed cues by providing a shared, evolving perception of the event and ICSs take pressure off the individual responder by distributing responsibility.

ICSs are typically set by the highest-ranking organization responding to the crisis, often at a federal level. More information on COPs and ICSs can be found in Chapter 4.

TECHNICAL MANAGEMENT

Black Swan crises may have disrupted the status quo *suddenly*, but the key to effective crisis response is *incrementalism*. This does not mean that leaders must respond slowly; rather they must stay ahead of problems as much as possible by working *progressively* toward a solution. A solution to a Black Swan crisis will not happen overnight.

Black Swan crises escalate rapidly and response strategies should outpace the event—to do this, leaders must keep their mental model rapidly expanding and evolving. Leaders must face new disruptions by projecting their revised understanding of the crisis back onto prior events and forward onto future events, improving comprehension of what has happened and making what has not yet happened more predictable. Leaders should keep in mind that their mission is to return to something more familiar as soon as possible.

The best way to gather information and respond incrementally and quickly is by recalibrating the response *iteratively*. This means taking an action, stepping back, and reflecting on its effects, and then acting again. This generates continuity and builds evaluation into the response process. It also provides information, which assists in a calmer, less chaotic, and more targeted response.

For a successful iterative response process, leaders should:

- Take small steps toward crisis mitigation
- Evaluate each step's impact and proceed accordingly
- Expect setbacks
- Overcome points of contention quickly

Leaders should not:

- Fear trial and error
- Overcommit to one exclusive crisis response

For a successful response, leaders should take small steps toward crisis mitigation, rather than sweeping decisions that require one large action. After a decision has been made and a step has been taken, leaders should evaluate its impact. Responders should be able to determine whether or not the step mitigated the crisis and can proceed accordingly. Leaders should expect setbacks. Extreme crisis response is not simple or linear; the path to success will be riddled with barriers. Leaders should, however, overcome points of contention quickly. Debates over decision-making should be resolved quickly taking even smaller steps in a certain direction can help resolve the dispute. Leaders should not fear trial and error. The only way to know if a certain response method will work is to try it. However, if a response does seem to be working, leaders should be cautious to not to overcommit to one exclusive response. Complex crises like Black Swans very rarely have one solution.

In Black Swan events, the crisis exceeds any responder's imagination. This unfathomable event means that basic response strategies must be used *in media res*, rather than deriving from prior preparation.

The first steps that responders should take are to:

- Make a list of operational priorities and supplies needed
- Assess the capabilities of all on-site responders
- Assess the capabilities of other organizations and leaders that might help
- Seek advice from technical experts, but do not allow this to delay decisions or fully guide the response
- Create joint plans with any internal and external actors based on a solid, realistic foundation
- Establish a regular battle rhythm (e.g., daily/weekly meetings)
- Keep pace with any changing situation
- Anchor decisions in facts when possible

To make a list of operational priorities and supplies, leaders must assess the crisis and quickly gather as much information as possible. For example, leaders at Fukushima determined that the nuclear reactors must be cooled to control a meltdown.

They can then assess the abilities of their teams to respond to this, before brainstorming and reaching out to other organizations that might be able to provide support. At Fukushima, leaders recognized that their teams could not control the radioactive materials that were leaking into the environment and that they needed federal and international support to control the radiation.

Technical experts can then be called into the crisis to evaluate the situation and provide insight into the best possible responses. However, these experts will likely act more slowly than the response time needed *in situ*—urgent decisions should not be delayed based on a lack of timely technical expertise. For example, the federal government did not intervene at Fukushima until March 12, 2011, one day after the initial earthquake. Until this point, on-scene actors had to control the nuclear reactors. The Japanese government later brought in outside assistance from the US.

Any plans that are made with internal and external actors should be built upon a solid, realistic foundation based on organizational capabilities and technical expertise when available. At Fukushima, the US and Japan developed a combined command system that integrated their respective response organizations—the US Department of Health and Human Services helped with radiation exposure information and the NRC advised the Japanese government on nuclear power issues while the Japanese military took control of cooling the nuclear reactors.

As the crisis progresses, a regular work, or "battle," rhythm should be established. This means setting consistent meetings so that all parties remain actively engaged with the crisis response. These meetings, and the decisions made at them, should keep pace with the evolving situation. These meetings should not be canceled at any cost, maintaining a battle rhythm is of utmost importance. For example, at Fukushima, leaders used the Hosono Process, or daily meetings to reconnect all involved response organizations.

Decisions should be anchored in facts when possible, meaning that choices can be traced back to data that supports it. However, technology should not be overly relied upon—this crisis event is most likely unprecedented, and computer models should be considered unreliable. At Fukushima, reliable data could not be gathered because IT infrastructure had cut communications between the crisis site and the government. This made it more difficult to respond to the crisis and coordinate among organizations.

Social amplification

Social amplification of risk in this crisis type is unique because Black Swan crises carry a larger political element than other crises. Political leaders are more inclined to take advantage of Black Swan crises for personal gain or political clout than they are other crisis types. Therefore, leaders must navigate political relationships most carefully when facing this event.

Politics and public relations management

Political issues must be managed just as technical issues are in a crisis. Black Swan events often draw global attention, and politics and public perception add layers of complexity to the response. Transboundary effects can pressure leaders to make decisions that do not align with technical realities, making important management crucial to an effective response. For example, at Fukushima, there was a significant miscommunication between plant operators and government regulators. The plant operators did not know how to communicate the changing conditions and the government did not consider how confusing the situation was *in situ*, leading to mistrust and excessively detailed instructions from the government to the on-site responders. Therefore, leaders must strategically liaise between the technical and political communities to mitigate confusion and improve the response.

As with all Black Swans, methods will vary based on the situation. However, generally, leaders should be aware of their roles as:

*   **Dispensers of hope to the community.** In Black Swan events, public sentiment is crucial to a continuous response, and strategically tempered enthusiasm can help sustain momentum.

    ☢ For example, the Japanese media was not prepared to cover a large-scale disaster and thus restricted information from the public. This led to widespread fear and loss of hope, and citizens turned to other (less reliable) information sources. Leaders missed an opportunity to garner public support by neglecting to form a relationship with the community.

*   **Inside sources of evolving information.** Sharing response strategies with the public can have the unintended consequence of overcommitment to a plan. This makes it more difficult to modify response approaches and adapt to future surprises. Leaders should be strategic in what information they share with the public.

    ☢ For example, leaders at Fukushima hoped to quell public fear by declaring that local rice and fish were safe to eat. However, scientists shortly discovered radiation contamination in the same food. This initial announcement created a false sense of safety and later caused increased panic among the public.

*   **Cultural liaisons and technical interpreters.** Black Swan events often call on leaders to work with organizations from different cultures, whether that is different nationalities or different areas of technical

expertise. Leaders must learn to work with people who have different customs and ways of thinking—these differences should be considered when problem-solving.

☢ For example, Japanese and American crisis response leaders had to work together to mitigate the Fukushima crisis. They worked with interpreters to overcome language differences and integrated teams with similar technical backgrounds to reduce barriers to understanding.

Social pressure placed on politicians is usually counterproductive, and relationships with politicians should be treated carefully. Therefore, leaders should still show extreme respect for distinguished experts and political leaders while prioritizing crisis response. At times, social considerations might outweigh technical considerations. When this happens, leaders must compensate by enhancing organizational response in other areas.

LEADERSHIP

In Black Swan crises, the response capabilities of leaders are secondary to the cause of the event, meaning that leaders cannot control the crisis and can only respond as best as possible. Leadership for a Black Swan requires a *warrior* ethos. Warrior leaders consistently transform, learn, and adapt to meet the demands of the crisis at hand.

Warrior leaders must be humble, cheerful, comforting, thoughtful, and reasonable. They must remain calm and collected in the face of the incomprehensible. These leaders' brains and emotions must be fully engaged, focused on overcoming felt emotions that might disrupt their response. They must remain flexible and fully in control. They must work against intuitive self-preservation and apply both wisdom and experience to make sense of a situation.

Leaders must listen in order to learn, help, and lead—if they do not listen closely to the people that they work with, they will become "bossy" rather than helpful. One way to develop strong leadership skills is to learn from other crisis leaders and focus on what makes them problem *solvers* rather than problem *creators*.

Leaders should remain as physically close to the response as possible—extreme crises require direction from experienced leaders and the further away a leader is from the event site, the less their involvement with and emotional attachment to the resolution and the responders. However, they must "keep one foot in the event and one foot out" both emotionally and psychologically to maintain perspective.

The role of a Black Swan crisis leader is to act as an intermediary to digest unpredictable raw material and transmute this into a more reliable end-product and solution. Leaders cannot do this without their response teams and outside organizations, so this section will largely focus on how to work with other responders in the midst of an unfathomable event. Leaders must understand that the event is more complex than they alone can manage, so they must work with their response team and others to mitigate the crisis.

Trust

Responders must trust their leaders. In Black Swan crises, there is often a point when workers are fearful of their lives and they reassess their level of trust in the leader. After that threshold comes a constant reassessment of trust in the leaders. Because leaders facing a Black Swan crisis cannot necessarily control the outcome, in these dangerous contexts, trust is a function of how well a leader performs. Supportive relationships between the leader and the responders, or loyalty, is key to a smooth response. Trust and loyalty go hand-in-hand when responding to a Black Swan crisis.

Leaders must consistently build trust throughout the response—team members will constantly reassess whether the leader is someone with whom they can work. Trust can be managed by "using the brakes and gas pedals of leadership," meaning that leaders know when to exert authority and when to pull back. Leaders can set a standard for hard work and dedication if they seek to have a long-term positive effect not only on the event resolution but also on the responders. Mentorship and relationship cultivation are crucial to crisis response.

Understanding the *what* and the *why*

One way that crisis leaders can help create an effective response is to ensure that their teams understand both *what* they need to do and *why* they are doing it. This may seem counterintuitive as Black Swan crises are high-pressure situations that allow little time for explaining and justifying commands. However, meaningful delegation can create a worthwhile response and prevent event escalation.

To ensure that teams understand *what* they are doing, leaders should:

- **Stay focused on the mission**—distractions will only cause confusion; leaders should not chase down "rabbit holes."
- **Give detailed directions**—ask responders to repeat back their orders to ensure understanding.
- **Assign specific tasks**—each individual should have ownership over a certain action/role that is based on their specific strengths or experience.
- **Know the organization's limitations and individual limitations**—understanding both an organizations and a team's capacities is crucial to avoiding a mismatch between a teams' ability and the task they are assigned when delegating response actions.
- **Address the *Casto Pandemonium Curve***—less information means more pandemonium, so leaders should gather as much information as possible.
- **Find ways to inject coherent information**—despite the lack of reliable data, leaders should make logical judgments based on experience.
- **Relay information in a way others can understand**—especially when dealing with non-technical personnel, leaders should be sure to use accessible terminology.
- **Be a technical interpreter**—assure superiors they will be getting a clear, accurate picture with straightforward recommendations.
- **Listen**—strive to understand what others are thinking and what constraints they perceive.
- To ensure that teams understand *why* they are doing certain tasks, leaders should:
- **Anchor decisions in facts**—make sure that key decisions are rooted in facts that can be readily shared with the team.
- **Never volunteer unfounded information**—supplying extraneous or unsubstantiated information can create confusion.
- **Strive to get the big picture**—problems are less likely to develop and solidify when everyone is working toward a common goal and vision.
- **Share the burden of uncertainty and doubt**—leaders should be transparent when things are unknown or unclear so that responders do not feel blindsided; when leaders are open about what they do not know, it will reduce general uncertainty.
- **Establish a shared understanding**—one way to establish a COP is by using a whiteboard and/or visual method that responders can return to often.

Responder relations

While it is key to ensure responders understand what to do and why they are doing it, leaders can only do this if they are skilled at *how* to communicate with their teams.

Leaders should:

- Allow responders to do their own sensemaking
- Empower responders to confront uncertainty
- Have patience with responders
- *Not* pretend to "know it all"
- *Not* act like they are "better than others"
- Congratulate small successes
- Continuously thank responders for their hard work
- Persuade rather than "boss"
- Use *intent-based* leadership
- Manage personality dynamics and internal politics
- Know when to speak up and when to back off
- Revise plans openly
- Help others develop leadership traits

Though leaders are ultimately working toward a shared understanding by developing a COP, they should allow responders to do their own sensemaking. This means including responders in the COP development process and answering any questions they may have about the situation. Leaders should also empower their teams to confront uncertainty. For example, leaders at Fukushima encouraged the fire department, the police, and the military to determine the best response team/method for dousing the nuclear reactor. These response teams were involved in the decision-making process and therefore better understood the crisis and their role in mitigating it.

Leaders should have patience with responders as they sensemake and confront uncertainty. Leaders should have faith that their teams are doing their best in the circumstances. For example, leaders in the control room understood that their teams were risking their lives to save their community. Leaders appealed to the operators' sense of duty and thanked them for their bravery.

Leaders should not pretend to "know it all" or that they are "better" than their teams. Humility is key to a strong leader/team dynamic. They should also prioritize using persuasive leadership techniques over "bossing." To counteract the negative felt emotions and provide some respite from dire circumstances, leaders should celebrate small successes and improvements as often as possible. This includes thanking responders for their hard work. For example, at Fukushima, when teams successfully completed tasks, leaders encouraged public acknowledgement with rounds of applause.

Leaders should base their organizational culture on common goals and the shared vision of success. This means actively curating a culture that focuses on *what* gets done rather than on *how* something gets done. For example, leaders at Fukushima were more focused on cooling the nuclear reactors than they were on sending helicopters to douse the building. This focus on the end goal granted leaders the freedom to modify their strategy and incorporate as many possible resources and teams as possible (i.e., utilizing the fire department and police for water on the ground).

Team dynamics and internal politics play a large role in helping or hindering a Black Swan crisis response. Leaders should emphasize managing personality dynamics and internal politics. To do this, leaders should know their teams and know who can work together well, but also when to speak up and when to pull back. For example, leaders at Fukushima were sympathetic to the fear and danger their teams were facing, as well as the need to remain humble. They lived with and ate meals with their teams, and every team member washed their dishes together.

Leaders should revise plans openly with their teams. This does *not* mean that leaders debate decisions publicly, but rather that once decisions have been made, changes in strategy are announced to the wider team. If time allows, leaders can explain the rationale behind strategy changes. For example, leaders set clear expectations that if the military's air-borne water cooling did not work, they would utilize fire departments as well. The involved response teams knew this criterion beforehand and were included in the process from ideation through to strategy change.

The strongest leaders help their teams develop leadership traits. These leaders are mindful of their directions and encourage responders to lead among themselves, even in the face of a Black Swan crisis. For example, during the Fukushima crisis, leaders shared the COP among responders at all levels so that they could develop sensemaking skills.

Black Swan crises are completely unfathomable—these crises surpass any event imagined or prepared for by the crisis response team. In this case, leaders can capitalize on common operational perspectives to make sense of the situation. Using this, they can consider the confidence and abilities of all teams to make decisions about the crisis response. The response to a Black Swan will likely be integrated, calling on multiple organizations to respond to the crisis. Leaders in Black Swan crises must be warriors. They must earn the trust of their teams to try to mitigate extreme, unprecedented disasters.

Black Swans will test a leader's capability to handle an extreme crisis. Using the strategies outlined above, leaders will be better prepared to take on this beast.

CHAPTER 9

Conclusion

The world today seems riddled with extreme crises. Globalization and technology have increased interconnectedness and triggered a chain reaction of disasters—from pandemics to armed conflict—serving as a potent reminder that no organization is immune from extreme crises.

From Black Elephants to Black Swans, no single leader can take on or solve a crisis. In the introduction of this handbook, leaders were encouraged to consider the real nature of their contribution: *What part of the crisis do you have power over? What problems can you work on directly? Who can be influenced? What information and resources can you access, or offer to others? If you can't fix it all—what can you do?*

This hand book provides a guideline with which to answer these questions based on crisis typology and a synthesis of crisis leadership academia. No crisis is the same or requires the same response, but if a leader can identify the elements of the crisis they are in, they can tailor their strategy to best respond and more quickly return their organization to the familiar.

Each crisis presents a different *situational context*—a combination of the triggering event and the capability of the organization to manage it. As crises increase in severity, so do their situational contexts. Responders must make sense of these contexts in order to respond; *sensemaking* strategies become more important as situations get more complex. Once responders have made sense of the situation, they are poised to make decisions and respond. *Decision-making* encompasses *what* responders choose to do and *crisis response* is *how* they do it. As crises become more extreme, decisions become more difficult and responses become more complex. *Leadership*, specifically, how leaders relate to their teams and move through a crisis, is important before, during, and after the crisis, regardless of type. Each crisis type has specific strategies to address the above stages; these strategies, when applied holistically, help to ensure that leaders are as equipped as possible for crisis management.

DOI: 10.4324/9781003289180-9

Although Black Elephant crises come as a surprise, leaders have information about the disaster before it happens and are able to take mitigative steps. They can influence the outcome by expanding their organization's capacities and building on their own experience, cooperating with their teams, and adapting their leadership to the demands of the situation.

Gray Rhino crises leave the leaders with perhaps the most "room for improvement." These crises are predictable, albeit not entirely preventable, and leaders have power to decrease their destruction if they take steps to recognize and mitigate the crisis before it happens. Gray Swan crises are similarly predictable but are far less probable. They leave leaders with catastrophic outcomes if they do not call on other organizations to assist with the response.

Black Swans are the rarest and most extreme crises. These events are unfathomable, catching leaders flat-footed, and unprepared. In these crises, leaders have no option but to become a warrior, integrating their response with other organizations and calling on their teams to unify in response.

The hope is that this handbook will be used *before* crises, to prepare organizations and leaders in case of an event, *during* crises, to guide the response and mitigate the chance of escalation, and even *after* crises, to help leaders evaluate their response and be more prepared for future events. Crises are only going to continue to become more complex; leaders must equip themselves with adequate resources to tackle them head on.

Index

Note: **Bold** pages refer to table.

Gray Rhino crises 41–43; Gray Swan crises 56–57
situational interpreters 7
situational leadership 64; *see also* leader/leadership
situation diagnosis 32
social amplification of risk framework 22, 82
solution aversion 49
space shuttle disasters 33
status quo 5, 61
subliminal 22–23
super-catastrophic crisis *see* Black Swan crises
Superstorm Sandy 43
supraliminal 22–23
surprise crisis 28, 35; *see also* Black Elephants crises
surprise events 6
Sweidan, A. 28
system failures 78

Taleb, N. N. 56, 69
technical interpreters 83–84
technical management 80–84
technologies 8
telling 65
transboundary crises 25–26
trust 24, 85

unidentified rhinos 42
unified decision-making 75–79; *see also* decision-making
unprecedented disasters 89; *see also* disasters
US Coast Guard 57
US National Weather Service 44, 49

value 8

white swan crises **13**, 13–14, 29, 68–69
Wucker, M. 41